The Quiz

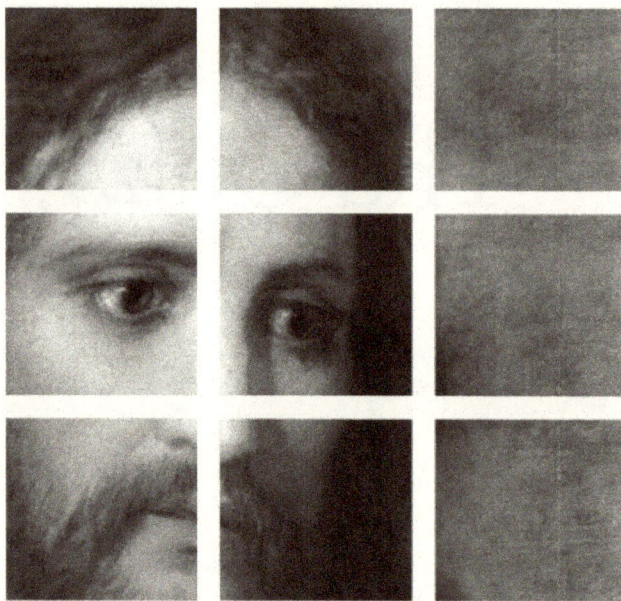

The Quiz

On the Nature
of the Incarnation of Jesus Christ

JONATHAN FLETCHER

Denver

ST MAXIMUS
SCRIPTORIUM

Published in the United States by
St. Maximus Scriptorium
14 Inverness Drive East, Suite F-160
Englewood, CO 80112
(303) 708-1632
www.stmaxscript.com

ISBN: 978-0-9838399-0-3

Library of Congress Cataloging-in-Publication Data is available upon
request.

Published in association with Samizdat Creative
samizdatcreative.com

Cover Design: White Bread Design
Cover Painting: from *Christ and the Rich Young Ruler* by Heinrich
Hofmann, 1889

Unless otherwise noted, all scripture references are taken from the
Ignatius Bible (RSV), 2nd Edition.

To my precious soul sister Penny

Contents

Preface

This project arose from a lunch with an Episcopal priest, Fletcher Montgomery, who was the rector of the church I was attending in 1995. My intention when I asked him to lunch was to discuss a set of questions I had developed, which I thought addressed some of the basics of who Jesus was when he was walking around among us around 2000 years ago. We talked about a number of things but never quite got around to what eventually became *The Quiz*. I asked him if he would be willing to write down his answers to the questions and send them to me, and he most graciously agreed.

The answers I received intrigued me. Some were what I would have expected. Other answers were far from my own poorly informed thoughts. I then proceeded to ask others the same questions—an Episcopal bishop, another Episcopal priest, an Eastern Orthodox priest, a Presbyterian pastor, and finally two Catholics—a nun and a priest—both of whom taught Christology at two different Catholic seminaries. The diversity of answers was nothing short of stunning. While I was unsure of what the "correct" answers were, one thing was clear—I was onto something. If the answers that Fletcher and others had given me had fallen neatly into well-defined and well-understood boxes, I might have thought that the whole project was trivial and not worth pursuing. In reality, just the opposite was the case. So I would have to thank

Fletcher for the stimulus to carry the project forward and especially for the courage to put his beliefs out there—for examination, possible edification and, of course the scariest prospect, possible criticism. I have found many who, when confronted by these possibilities, have backed away. While I am confounded by this response to an opportunity to share one's beliefs regarding Jesus Christ, I now understand that one's first reaction to these questions could be quite varied. I have experienced disdain, curiosity, delight, fear, and just plain horror. Let me address each of these responses, because I think they shed some important light on how we see *our understanding* of Jesus.

Before I do this, however, I should lay out some ground rules, since I have discussed *The Quiz* with folks from a wide range of Christian denominations. This is in essence a Christian quiz. It is focused on understanding the most basic elements of the Incarnation, the "enfleshment" or the way in which humanity and divinity coexisted in Jesus Christ while he was on earth. Because of the influence a denominational perspective has on the way a person approaches these questions, it seems edifying to allude to these denominational roots to see if they inform the larger picture of how people think about Jesus. Please know that we all are struggling to grasp the greatest mystery that mankind has encountered in our entire history—how God could become man and offer us God's own life in the process. This struggle, in fact, has been going on since the Apostles themselves grappled with their own understanding of the Jesus in their midst. And this struggle has continued to this day, not only in individual lives, but also in the halls of the great Christian bodies. The early Ecumenical Councils struggled mightily to articulate the boundaries of this mystery in order to constrain believers within bounds consistent with the teachings of Jesus and the Apostles. The eastern and western parts of the early Church struggled with each other over basic issues concerning the Incarnation until the Great Schism of A.D. 1054 when the Church split into the Roman Catholic Church and the Eastern Orthodox Church. Finally, the ultimate struggle culminated in the Protestant Reformation that began in the early 1500s and resulted in a profound divergence on many fundamental issues regarding what happened 2000 years ago and what it means for us today.

So if I refer to a denomination in the discussion of this project and particularly to certain kinds of answers that were given to the questions on *The Quiz*, let me assert that it is only in an attempt to get closer to a deeper truth. All of us who see ourselves on a journey toward God through belief in Jesus Christ, first and foremost, are to be known by our love for one another and not by our theological correctness. It is hoped and strongly believed, however, that theological correctness does indeed inform how we love one another, and thus one of the most important things we do may be to try our best to figure out and clearly articulate who Jesus was. In that vein, let's address some of the basic attitudes that have been expressed by those confronted with the questions on *The Quiz* and the answers offered here.

The Questions

Why might one have disdain for these questions? In the first place, many Christians have an understanding of Jesus that stresses his intimate relationship with God, but may not stress Jesus' humanity. One can fall into this bias without totally discounting his humanity—an understanding that would clearly be considered antithetical to the Apostolic Christian message.

What is most interesting is that one's response to *The Quiz* can often point out precisely this kind of bias, which could be just as damaging as the utter denial of his humanity. Typically this kind of response reflects the idea that the questions are silly, irrelevant and equivalent to the ancient question of "how many angels can dance on the head of a pin?" This may be the best place to state unequivocally, don't you be fooled. These questions are much more sophisticated than they appear, and they have the capacity to uncover many errors in belief, as well as to demonstrate many profound truths regarding the nature of Jesus Christ. The answers you give will go a long way in uncovering your own biases and possible traps you may have fallen into, just as my own answers to the questions may uncover my own biases and traps into which I may have plummeted.

Why might one view the questions on The Quiz *with curiosity?* In many instances these kinds of questions may have never been asked before. The nature of the Savior of the world has been taken to be something essentially inaccessible, save for the professional clergy and those involved with the teaching of theology in universities and seminaries. Most of us are brought up to believe that there are correct answers and incorrect answers, and that usually only those who have studied the subject have access to the correct ones. The truth is, however, that the correct answers are often the ones related to common sense and are accessible to anyone with modest intellectual powers, myself included. Jesus often confounded the intellectual aristocracy and related naturally to those who were willing to take him at face value—particularly children. As a matter of fact, he admonished us all to approach the truth of his teaching as little children. It is not that there are not correct or orthodox answers, since that is the point of the exercise. It is that what many believe are the correct answers are in fact not, and what seems too simple to be true is in fact true.

Why might one delight in the questions on The Quiz? There may be many reasons. I will give one example. At a conference on Christian education, I was sitting at a table with an Episcopal priest and friend of mine, Blaney Pridgen. I mentioned *The Quiz,* and he immediately lit up with delight at the prospect of being challenged in this way. He encouraged me to give him a question. As I started to ask some of the questions, he again took great delight in offering his answers. In fact, he was one of the few people who "made a hundred," if one accepts the answers presented here as the correct ones.

Why did he take such delight in addressing these questions about Jesus? I would suggest the reason is that he took great delight in Jesus himself. Once one understands the amazing gift that has been given to us in Jesus Christ, one takes great delight in talking about him and engaging in meaningful dialogue about who he was and what he was about. I am reminded of Jeremiah here:

> If I say, "I will not mention him, or speak any more in his name," there is in my heart as it were a burning fire shut up in my bones, and I am weary with holding it in, and I cannot. (Jeremiah 20:9)

In the end, the people who were willing to answer these questions unhesitatingly and with a certain amount of delight were clearly those who were confident in their faith— not necessarily confident in the *answers,* but confident in their *faith.* The problem, of course, is that few of us are confident in our faith and in our understanding of the great mystery of the Incarnation. One of the goals of *The Quiz* is to dispel much of the apparent complexity and to uncover the accessibility of Jesus.

Why might one feel a sense of fear when asked these basic questions about Jesus? Again, the reasons may be complex, but I would suggest that one reason might be the fear of being wrong. Even though we as Christians should be living our lives on the basis of our understanding of who Jesus was (and *is*), we fail to see the imperative to find out the truth. Answers that take us out of that comfort zone, by definition, make us feel *uncomfortable*. Even though we are told repeatedly by Jesus that the "truth will set us free," we generally adhere to the idea that *our delusions keep us safe*. We hold onto them like a baby holds onto his or her blankie, no matter how smelly the thing becomes. We are attached to our own perceptions and are therefore blocked from a larger and fuller truth that will take us to a much better place.

Another reason one might feel a sense of fear is that one might be held accountable, especially if one is in a position of academic prestige or ecclesial authority. While I believe the answers in many instances are simple and based on common sense, they are easily misconstrued. To some, a simple answer to one question might imply an overall belief system that in fact is not orthodox. Simple answers can be twisted and used to support an erroneous theology. One professor looked at the questions and demurred from answering them on the basis that a book could (and implicitly *should*) be written on each question to ensure that all the possible theological holes were plugged. I am most aware of the traps associated with simple answers. But that does not make the simple answers wrong; it just means that we all need to take care to see those answers in a broader context of our full understanding of Jesus. The answers may be simple: the explanations may not only be complex but full of wonder and mystery.

Finally, why might one look at questions on The Quiz *with horror?* Well, as the questions become increasingly bolder toward the end of *The Quiz*, they require increasingly bolder answers. It may very well appear that the implied answers are not only wrong but massively contrary to your own beliefs. I recall someone who looked at *The Quiz* and then took it to her priest for comment. She responded that she and the priest thought that the questions were not only misguided but also dangerous. She could come to this conclusion only if she felt that the answers being sought were not only erroneous, but horribly so. Once we are able to look at the questions objectively, considering the wonder of the *correct* answers instead of the *presumed* answers, I hope we are able to see the power of this understanding of Jesus.

The Answers

Another angle on all of this relates to the answers. Even if one takes seriously the *questions*, one could have a variety of responses to the *answers* that are offered here. This is a good time for a personal confession. I am a Catholic—a relatively new one—which makes me particularly obnoxious and pushy. Furthermore, this means that the answers I take to be "correct" arise out of a process of scriptural interpretation and doctrinal development that has taken place over the past 2000 years. The role that the Church plays in even attempting to articulate answers to the deepest questions regarding Jesus is, to me, critical. Without what Catholics call the magisterium, the teaching authority of the Church, we could have no correct answers, only opinions. This whole exercise would devolve into a statement of what *I* thought were the correct answers. I am not in the least interested in putting forth *my* answers; I am only interested in a truth that transcends my own capacity for understanding this great mystery. I am continually astounded by the way the pieces of Scripture fit together to form a whole that could not have been dreamed up by one theologian or one person with a messianic complex. To read the Gospel writers, as well as Paul, Peter, the Church Fathers—the ones who first attempted to fit the puzzle together—and finally the writings of the great Councils, is to see not a monument to the ingenuity and creativeness of individuals, but a breathtaking reflection of the deepest truths of God and man. No one could or would have dreamed up a story this confounding. It is like looking at a space shuttle and thinking that it arose out of some process of probabilistic chance. The more one contemplates the amazing systems that must function together to make the thing work, the more one realizes that it must be the product of the highest mental capacity of man. The story of our salvation through the life, death and resurrection of Jesus Christ takes this kind of thinking to another level. The more we contemplate the story, the more we come to the conclusion that it is of God. And if it is of God, it is worthy of our time and energy to wrestle with what it all means.

The Methodology

Finally, let me say a word about methodology. There are two issues here: (1) my understanding of orthodoxy or "right belief," and (2) what we might call "cognitive" approaches taken toward some of the challenging issues raised by the questions on *The Quiz*. In other words the correctness of the answers and the way we think about arriving at the answers.

As I mentioned above, I am unabashedly taking a Catholic perspective. Clearly what one takes to be the orthodox answers will depend on one's religious background. At the beginning of the project, I was in search of consistency in the answers I sought from others. Not finding that, I looked for consistency within my own faith, which was at that time Episcopalian. No consistency there. This consistency was also difficult to find as I searched other Protestant denominations. While one might expect consistency in the hierarchical and doctrinally tight Catholic Church, I was gratified when I found it. At least I could clearly define the answers from one perspective. Although since then I have found much disparity in the beliefs of individual Catholics, the one constant is the understanding within the Catholic Church as reflected in the *Catechism of the Catholic Church*[1] and a host of writings that the Church holds to be orthodox. The very fact that there is a "Congregation for the Doctrine of the Faith"[2] means that the Church takes consistency seriously. Consequently, I am constrained to take as my benchmark for orthodoxy the teachings of the Catholic Church and will use the word "Church" with a capital "C" in this sense. Having said that, I would ask the readers who are not Catholic to consider what is their

---

1 Second Edition, *Libreria Editrice Vaticana* (1997), 904 pp.

2 This is the office in the Vatican tasked with vetting teachings and doctrine both inside and outside the Catholic Church. It used to be called the Supreme Sacred Congregation of the Holy Office (established in 1904) and before that the Supreme Sacred Congregation of the Roman and Universal Inquisition (established in 1542) that got such a horrid reputation in its special manifestation in Spain (established in 1480) under the control of the Spanish monarchy. The general approach to dealing with heresy began with a number of Papal Inquisitions from the 12th century. The story is complex and worth reading about, if one wants to understand the interface of secular power and the legitimate concern of the Church for orthodoxy in its teachings. Much was learned at a high price.

own meaning that they might attach to the term "Church." I would challenge you to think of the sources of authority in your own Christian traditions that would play the same role as my own understanding of the word "Church" and see where they take you. If you are from a "Sola Scriptura" (only Scripture) tradition, you might even try substituting the word "Scripture."

Regarding the second point about methodology, you will notice that periodically I will comment on various ways of thinking about or approaching the questions. They might seem to be digressions, but I would assert that these notes may be of considerable help in understanding how to attack these and other questions that inevitably come up in any discussion of complex issues. I hope that when you have worked your way through the questions, the proposed answers and the methodological notes, you will be better equipped to do your own work with challenging questions and the answers proposed by yourself and others.

Introduction

Who do you say that I am?

Before we begin this journey to a clearer understanding of the Incarnation of Jesus Christ, we are compelled to ask a fundamental question. Why do we even care who Jesus was and is? Why is he even important? Jesus was very clear on the need for Peter and the rest of the Apostles—as well as you and me—to answer the question, *"Who do you say that I am?"*[3] Is Jesus just a nice guy? An interesting historical figure? A charlatan? A myth? A fraud? A great teacher? A prophet? Or the son of the living God?

While most people who call themselves Christians take this importance for granted, it may be useful to re-examine this fundamental question of his importance. What we are looking for, as we wend our way through this life, whether we believe in heaven or not, is *life itself.* But *what kind of life* are we talking about? Is the quality of life best expressed as a kind of continuum—from a poor excuse for a life to life in its highest form? Is a murderer somehow failing at life, while a saint is somehow living life to its fullest? If we assume this kind of continuum exists and that goodness trumps badness, then we must start to look for guidelines—markers that indicate how to judge goodness and badness. In other words, we

---

3   Matthew 16:13

might look for a model.

If we were to ask who is a model of goodness, some might say Peter Pan or Santa Claus or maybe even Abe Lincoln. Some might say Moses or the Buddha. Some might point to Mahatma Gandhi or Mother Teresa. Whatever the yardstick, we somehow feel compelled to find the highest and best, because to fall short of the highest and best is to fall short of *life itself*. The underlying premise of *The Quiz* is that this Jesus of Nazareth is at least worthy of our consideration as a good model for our lives and at most is the absolute highest and best, the alpha and omega, the beginning and the end, better than any other.

Here is another way to think of it. Each of us has something that we hold to be of paramount importance. It could be our spouse or our children. It could be money, power or prestige. It could be alcohol, drugs, self-absorbed sex or some other form of addictive pursuit. It could be self-indulgence or an obsession with another person, like the charismatic leader of a group (some would call this a cult). Whatever you hold to be of ultimate importance could be viewed as your *god*. If you hold love and truth to be of ultimate importance, then the model of love and truth could be called, for you, God. While this certainly does not exhaust the idea that for some Jesus is God, it is at least a start at understanding why he might be so important to so many people. Perhaps you could think of it this way. Those who think Peter Pan represents the highest and best would be called *Peterpanians*. Those who think Mickey Mantle is the ultimate model for their lives would be *Mantelians* and so on. Those who think Jesus Christ represents the highest and best are called *Christians*. For these folks, understanding Jesus is of primary importance. *The Quiz* is therefore our attempt to explore the depth of the importance of Jesus as our model.

Finally, we have talked about the Incarnation as the en-fleshment of God—God taking on human flesh and blood in order to show us the way back to God. The importance of God becoming flesh is indicated by one of the Church Fathers, Tertullian (A.D. 160–220), who called the flesh "the hinge of salvation,"[4] meaning all of salvation is mediated by the flesh and blood of the humanity of Jesus Christ. Everything that takes place to move us from where we are to a new and better place is somehow facilitated by the flesh. So while we may envision our journey back to God as primarily spiritual, our physicality is an essential ingredient to the process. We act through our bodies and we are acted upon through our bodies. There is no way to divorce our spirit from our bodies. This is why Christianity is such a powerful way to God, because it recognizes the essential goodness of our physicality, breathing life back into not only our spirit, but also our bodies. To the extent that the characteristics of God are incompatible with this physicality, they are not a part of Christ's Incarnation and our own journey, which follows his path laid out for us through the Incarnation. Our challenge is not to have Christ's divinity *swamp* his humanity to the extent that it would undermine the way our salvation is brought about—through the flesh. We could also say that we do not want his humanity to *swamp* his divinity to the detriment of the same process through the power and activity of God. This fruitful image helps us keep both divinity and humanity in proper perspective as we try to arrange the pieces of the Incarnation "puzzle" into a more complete and accessible picture.

---

4   *On the Resurrection of the Flesh*, Ante-Nicene Fathers, Roberts, Alexander, ed., Hendrickson Publishers, 1999, p. 551.

While this whole body of thought could be seen as a *puzzle*, it is in actuality much more than this. It is a *mystery*. A puzzle is something to be solved; a mystery is something to be entered into and lived. While I believe there are aspects of each in our efforts to understand the Incarnation of Jesus Christ, the distinction between a *puzzle* and a *mystery* is a very important one. On the one hand, the Incarnation can be seen as a puzzle. We have the Gospel writers, who themselves were trying to piece together the events of Jesus' life into some larger and more profound context. How did the actions of Jesus relate to those of Moses, Abraham, David, and Isaiah? How did the Gospel writers understand the life of Jesus in a larger time frame? What are the implications of the life of Jesus for the future? The answers to these questions require one to see the Incarnation as a piece of a larger puzzle. Yet on the other hand, one of the greatest understandings to come from this process is that the Incarnation is not something to be explicitly "solved," such that once you fit the pieces together everything is perfectly clear and analytically tight. There is always a gap that cannot be bridged by rational thought alone. We call this part of the puzzle a *mystery*. At every turn we might seek a concrete unequivocal answer to a question, but we often find a paradox blocking the road. As we will see, we must learn not only to endure the paradoxes but also to appreciate that often the deepest truths are found embedded in unsolvable paradox. We are forced to appreciate that ultimately they are not a puzzle to be solved but a mystery to be lived into. This is not to say we should throw rationality out the window, as our rational thought is a critical tool in entering the mystery. The analogy I like to use is that of a diving board. Just as we walk out and stand at the *end* of the diving board in order to dive in, we exercise our rational thought until it takes us as far as we can go *rationally* before we dive into the mystery by faith.

While the questions on *The Quiz* may appear simple on the surface, the underlying implications of the answers are profound, often complex, and deeply mysterious. The problem, therefore, is that for an answer to be meaningfully understood, one must make certain distinctions regarding the words one uses not only in *answering* the question being addressed, but also in *understanding* the question as well. One such fundamental distinction regards the name and person of *Jesus*. What do we mean when we refer to Jesus? Unfortunately, to answer this we must be a bit circular, because *The Quiz* itself is intended to address this very question. Ironically, we can't even begin to answer questions regarding who Jesus was without having some common understanding of the Jesus of whom we speak. Here is a stab at setting out a statement for which the name *Jesus* will be shorthand without giving away any answers to the questions. In short, when I use the name *Jesus* within the context of the questions on *The Quiz*, I am referring to a man who lived 2000 years ago; who was the Son of God, a divine person, and the Second Person of the Trinity; who was divine by nature and who from conception took on a human nature and freely chose to operate on earth as a human being. One way to test what I mean by the word Jesus in the context of any question is to imagine yourself walking up to him in first century Palestine when he was in his earthly ministry and asking *him* the question. The answer that you think he would have given you is the answer you should give. Our job as we work our way through these answers is to try to clarify who he really was and what those answers would have been.[5] Remember we *are*

---

5   This kind of technique might be called a heuristic—something that

talking about a mystery here, but our objective is to make the mystery so accessible that it has the power to change our lives. If we only dwell on the mystery, without wrestling with the concrete reality of the Incarnation, we will have missed the whole point of the Christ event. The Incarnation is about making concrete that which was *simply mystery*:

> That which was from the beginning, which we have heard, which we have seen with our eyes, which we have looked upon and touched with our hands, concerning the word of life—the life was made manifest, and we saw it, and testify to it, and proclaim to you the eternal life which was with the Father and was made manifest to us—that which we have seen and heard we proclaim also to you, so that you may have communion with us; and our communion is with the Father and with his Son Jesus Christ. And we are writing this that our joy may be complete.[6] (1 John 1:1–5)

The Quiz is not the place to elucidate all the subtleties of the language being used. I would simply ask you to recognize that if you don't buy into some of the concepts assumed in the following discussions, it may be because you don't yet fully understand them. These are difficult ideas

points the way to a solution without itself being an integral part of the "chain of evidence."

6   As you can see, I have substituted the word "communion" for the word "fellowship' that is used in the RSV translation. It was pointed out to me that the Greek word *koinonia* implies a deeper kind of union that is not captured by the modern way in which we use the word "fellowship."

and concepts, ones that have been discussed and debated for nearly 2000 years. With this in mind, have fun, knowing that in the end you may discover you understand more than you first thought. The fact of the matter is this Jesus, who many think is the highest and best, is much more accessible than many of us have ever dreamed.

So here we are, on the threshold of an adventure. I would suggest that you simply make a copy of the questions in *The Quiz* or download them from the website (www.thequiz.stmaxscript.com) and answer the questions using your most basic common-sense understanding of the earthly life Jesus led. You may want to give *The Quiz* to family, friends, or even a Sunday school class, discussing the pros and cons of your answers. Be sure to take the quiz before moving on to the rest of the chapters in the book, since only after you have struggled with your own answers are you fully prepared to read on and wrestle with what many believe to be the orthodox answers.

The compelling question Jesus asked Peter—"*Who do you say that I am?*"—is the same question he poses to each of us. How we answer this question forms the spiritual grounding of how we live here on earth.

May this little quiz help you along this wondrous journey.

The Quiz

Here is a little quiz for your edification and enjoyment. Its purpose is to stimulate your thinking about some things that may seem trivial on the surface, but in actuality, cut right to the core of who Jesus was and how accessible his very being is to each of us. It is also fun to see how your answers may differ from those close to you, your spouse and friends. Talking about it over breakfast or lunch is good. Don't worry about being wrong. Most everyone is, in one way or another, since this apparently innocuous quiz is anything but. So have fun, knowing this may be the beginning of a glorious and transformative journey. I certainly hope so.

By the way, feel free to include any thoughts or insights as to why you answered the questions the way you did.

Considering the three *all*-encompassing qualities of God the Father:

> Omnipotent—all powerful
> Omniscient—all knowing
> Omnipresent—present everywhere, all the time:

> 1. Which of these qualities did Jesus possess when he walked the earth?

2. Of which of these did the Son empty himself when he became "incarnate"?

3. After the resurrection and before the ascension, which of these qualities did Jesus possess?

4. In his earthly ministry, was Jesus the source of his own authority?

5. As a Christian, do you have any authority?

6. If so, what is the source of that authority?

7. Did Jesus know how to play golf?

8. If Jesus had known how to play golf, could he have made a hole-in-one whenever he wanted to?

9. Name one human being who was *perfect* in the eyes of the Father.

10. Do you consider Jesus to have been *perfect*?

11. If you consider Jesus to have been perfect, how much of that perfection has been offered to us as humans?

12. Could Jesus have said "no" to the will of the Father? For example, could he have refused to go to the Cross?

13. Under what circumstances, if any, could you walk on water?

14. Under what circumstances, if any, could you raise someone from the dead?

15. If we say that Jesus was "one substance" with the Father, what is his relationship to us?

16. If Jesus was "fully human and fully divine," does this mean that his humanity was somewhat different from ours?

17. How good can you be?

18. Can you be without sin?

19. If you cannot be without sin, which sins are considered acceptable to the Father?

20. In light of the death and resurrection of Jesus, are you still a slave to original sin?

21. Did Jesus have faith? How much?

22. How much faith can you have?

23. How much glory has been offered to you?

24. How much divinity has been offered to you?

25. Is it possible for you to be one with the Father as Jesus was one with the Father?

26. How much like Jesus are you called to be?

27. How is Jesus different from you?

28. If someone saw in you the goodness of Jesus and fell down on their knees and said, "My Lord and my God," what would be your response?

29. Can you *be* God? If you answer in the affirmative, in what sense do you mean it?

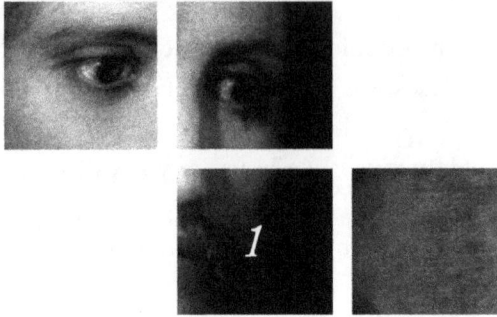

Which of These Qualities

Considering the three all-encompassing qualities of God the Father:

Omnipotent—all powerful
Omniscient—all knowing
Omnipresent—present everywhere, all the time

Which of these qualities did Jesus possess when he walked the earth?

L et's start this out by asserting something fundamental about the Incarnation. While the intent of this book is not to treat exhaustively the arguments for a given answer, it is important at least to set down some basic principles. It is certainly true that some who consider themselves scholars in the area of Christology (the study of Jesus Christ) would argue that the answers presented here are not only wrong but pure heresy. Their objective would be to preserve some aspect of the Incarnation that they feel the answers jeopardize.

On the other hand, others who are not the least bit informed of the subtle arguments concerning the nature of the Incarnation would argue from a purely common-sense point of view and concur with the answers given here. In other words, we might say that some could be wrong for the right reasons and some could be right for the wrong reasons. The right and wrong of it all is therefore a tricky issue. Let me assert that my intention is not to offer what *I think* are the correct answers, but to explore the purely orthodox answers that the Apostles would have given and that the Church would support as a result of 2000 years of continued doctrinal clarification. These answers are intended to open the way for us as individuals to access the complete breadth and scope of the salvation inaugurated through the Incarnation. With this in mind, let's have at it.

Omnipotence

We need to get a grasp of what we mean by the term "omnipotence." When we say that God is omnipotent, we mean that he[7] is all (omni) powerful (potent). That means that if God were to decide[8] to end the universe, poof, it is gone. The 400 billion stars in the Milky Way Galaxy, of which our sun is just one, and the 200 billion galaxies that comprise our universe—poof—gone. To say that Jesus was omnipotent when he walked the earth is to say that he, as a human

---

7   I use the masculine only for convenience, recognizing that God transcends our earthly gender distinctions. I will also use a lower case "h" in the word "he" when referring both to God the Father and to Jesus in order to avoid any implicit theological issues.

8   Note that the way God "decides" probably bears little resemblance to the human decision-making process. We have little understanding of how the transcendent God decides, so the use of the term is limited to a result rather than a process.

being, could have gone "poof," and made the whole universe go away—including his incarnate self.

What do I mean by saying that Jesus was a *human being*? With the Council of Nicaea in A.D. 325, the Church asserted that Jesus was a divine *person* with both a divine and a human *nature*. To say that Jesus was a *human being* is to capture an important aspect of the Church's formula that all of Jesus' actions were constrained by his humanity. He was a human entity, a man, if you will, who walked and talked and bled and died just like you and me. The connection to his divine nature, which in fact did possess all the qualities of God, is more complex. This union of natures, called the *hypostatic union*, was not clarified until the Council of Chalcedon in A.D. 451, and even then the statement needed further critical clarification at the Third Council of Constantinople in A.D. 680. It is a true mind bender and is not for anyone faint of heart or intellect, but I hope we can do what we need to do without wading too deeply into the understanding of these complexities.

Now, why might one think that Jesus was omnipotent? It could be because he *was* God. It also could be partly because he showed his divinity through a host of miracles that clearly operated outside the normal laws of nature. How could he do that if he did not possess extraordinary powers? How and why do we call him God and then proceed to strip him of one of the most basic characteristics of God—namely, that God can do whatever God wants? This is precisely why the early Church had such problems with the Incarnation, because so many aspects of it challenge our intuition.

On the other hand, remember the Apostles' starting point was an encounter with someone they perceived to be a *man*. It took some convincing before Peter could articulate one of the most profound confessions of faith when asked by Jesus, "Who do you say that I am?" His response resonates throughout time and space: "You are the Messiah, the son of the living God." And recall Jesus' response: "Blessed are you, Simon son of Jonah! For flesh and blood has not revealed this to you, but my Father in heaven" (Matthew 16:15–17). In other words, there is no way to comprehend (with the mind) or even apprehend (with the heart) this profound truth simply by some rational argument based on the flesh and blood actions of Jesus. It requires an understanding derived from faith. With this in mind we can also say that a complete understanding of the Incarnation and how the pieces of the puzzle/ mystery fit together is beyond our human mental capacity. While we can set some boundaries defining what is false, we will always fail to fully expound what is true.

So we are left with the same dilemma that faced the first followers of Jesus, as well as the early Church. *Who was the incarnate Son of God, Jesus Christ?* Here might be an alternative answer. Everything Jesus did was consistent with being human, while in his deepest essence he *was* the Son of God. He was constrained to work through his humanity to accomplish his mission. What the followers of Jesus saw was a *man*. The characteristics that were manifest were human characteristics. Assuming that he lived today, here are a few questions that might help to focus our thinking. Could he leap tall buildings in a single bound? Could he bend steel bars with his bare hands? Could he stand at the middle of a basketball court blindfolded with his back to the net, throw the basketball over his head backwards and make a basket, nothing but net, 500 times in a row? Could he take a baseball, throw it around the earth three times and make it travel out around Mars 10 times, return to earth and come across the plate low and outside for a strike, just clipping the corner of the strike zone? What he could do was turn water into wine, still the raging storm, walk on water, heal the sick, cast out demons, make the lame walk, and raise the dead. We find that as our vision of omnipotence expands,[9] our ease of ascribing that characteristic to one who came to be as we are seems to vanish in the mist, and we are left with something far more compelling—a man who is constrained as we are and still shows us a window into the life of God. This should become much clearer as we go along.

Omniscience

The question here is whether Jesus knew (science) everything (omni), but let's be clear about what that means. To know everything would literally be to have the mind of God, meaning that he would not only know every fact that ever existed or will exist throughout all time, but also understand the relationships between all things, past, present and future, in the same way that God would understand them.

Why might we assert that Jesus was omniscient? He certainly knew some things that seemed to transcend the normal bounds of human knowing. He told the woman at the well all about herself, astounding her with this special knowledge. He knew about his special relationship to the Father. He knew about his own death and alluded to his resurrection. This kind of knowledge doesn't seem quite "natural." So it would make sense that many of his followers would ascribe to him the natural ongoing knowledge of whatever he wanted to know—that he could know *everything* if he wanted

---

9   This classical philosophical trick is called *reductio ad absurdum* (reduction to the absurd) and means that we keep pressing the limits of an argument until the argument becomes absurd.

to. If he were not simply "play acting," then we would have to conclude that he *did* know everything and exhibited that knowledge whenever he wanted to. This understanding of Jesus is all too easy and seems to agree with our common sense. It is therefore no wonder that many today believe this to be true of him.

The problem here is that for Jesus to be truly human and have the mind of God at the same time, he would have to have an infinite number of neurons, and each neuron would have to function with infinite capacity and efficiency. In other words, he would not have a human brain like you and I have, but some kind of infinitely large, infinitely efficient brain that somehow would emulate the totally unlimited "mind of God." Either that, or he could tap into the mind of God at will; but even then he would have to filter out the infinitely large amount of information in order to end up with some kind of "understanding" that could fit into a finite brain and be articulated using finite faculties of mental processing and speech. While we normal humans use about 10% of our brains to process and store information, and modern desktop computers have processing and storage capabilities that far exceed at least some functionality of the human brain, omniscience would have to far exceed even the largest supercomputers. I am trying to show that infinite omniscience is both physically and functionally incompatible with finite humanity that has a finite brain with finite functionality. For Jesus to be human and show us what humanity is intended to look like, we should have considerable trouble ascribing to him characteristics that are infinitely different from our own. The challenge here is that we are trying to compare the finite with the infinite, and as you can see, that really doesn't work very well.

If we play the same game that we played above and stretch the concept of omniscience, we might get some clarity. Even if these challenges mentioned above could be satisfied, we would have to understand omniscience as expressed by a human being as the ability to know all facts and figures of past, present and future. How many atoms are in the universe? What is the speed of light to 450 decimal places? How do you build a super computer with 1×10^{23} teraflops?

If indeed Jesus was constrained by his humanity in the area of knowledge, he would not have known what an atom was in the sense that we mean it today, complete with quarks and neutrinos and hadrons and bosons and fermions and positrons and on and on. He would not have known anything about the wave/particle nature of light, let alone how fast it travels. And he, along with most of us, would not have known what flops are (floating point operations per second), let alone what the scientific notation of 1×10^{23} might mean or the fact that this number of teraflops is an astronomically high processing rate, far beyond what we can even envision or what might be theoretically possible. Once we get a better handle on just what omniscience might look like, we begin to demure from trying to ascribe it to one who was called *a man*. What he could do was to know the life of the woman at the well, to know his own mission as the Son of God who came to give the world eternal life, to know as intimately as possible for any human being the nature of his Heavenly Father, to know his own fate as he pursued the Cross of salvation, and so on. We thus point toward an understanding of the Incarnation that is much more compelling for us than a person who could do whatever he wanted and knew everything. The way in which Jesus worked through his humanity to show us the face of God is one of the great mysteries of life, and our understanding of his knowledge is crucial to our understanding of the Incarnation as a whole.

Omnipresent

The question here is whether Jesus was present in all places at all times while he was on the earth. The one thing most people would agree on is that Jesus was, in fact, constrained by place and time. The very definition of "Incarnation" seems to put a certain stamp on this dilemma. While we have trouble understanding Jesus' limitations associated with *doing* and *thinking*, we seem to be more secure in asserting limitations associated with his state of being in the world; that is to say, when he was here, he was here, and when he was there, he was there. When he was visiting Mary and Martha in Bethany, he was not giving a sermon in the temple in Jerusalem at the same time. The whole New Testament would be a confused mess if there had not been some kind of linear chronology based on the fact that Jesus was not in more than one place at a time. Place and time worked for him just as they work for us. It is not clear why some folks are so quick to limit him in one characteristic of God but so reluctant to limit him in others. Now after the resurrection, we have some new rules, but we will get to that later.

Why would it matter whether or not he was omnipotent, omniscient, and omnipresent? What difference does it make to us? Here is the point: If he were any of these, he would have been infinitely different from you or me. Clearly we mere mortal human beings are neither omnipotent nor intended to be, neither omniscient nor intended to be, neither omnipresent nor intended to be. These things are not part of our humanity. When we are called by God to do something, our response is constrained by our natural human limitations.

That is all we have. (We will talk about miracles later.) The point of the Incarnation is that God meets us where we live, with the very same limitations we experience. He not only shows us what it looks like to utilize those limitations in the eternal life of God, but also gives us the means of doing it ourselves—he *is* the means of doing it. This theme will be repeated over and over as we address the "what does it matter" question at the end of each topic. In general, it matters if God really meets us where we live and does not just pretend to "play" human but really *is* human. His complete humanity makes him a *human being*. This humanity does not limit or diminish his divinity; it merely asserts that while he was walking around, he functioned as a man—one in intimate relationship with the Father—but a man nonetheless.

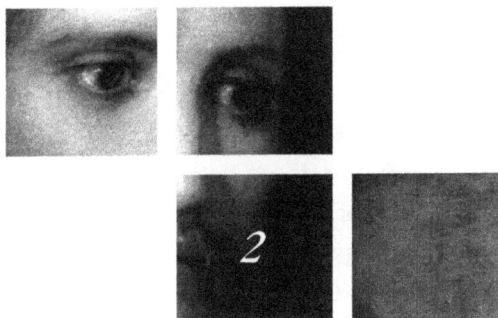

The Son Emptied Himself

Of which of these characteristics did the Son empty himself
when he became "incarnate"?

A s with many of the questions on *The Quiz*, this question explores more deeply what we discussed in chapter one. Here we take into account Paul's statement in his letter to the Philippians in which he asserts the following:

> Let the same mind be in you that was in Christ
> Jesus, who, though he was in the form of God,
> did not regard equality with God as something
> to be grasped, but emptied himself, taking the
> form of a slave, being born in human likeness.
> And being in human form, he humbled him-
> self and became obedient to the point of death—
> even death on a cross. (Philippians 2:5–8)

The Greek word for this emptying is *kenosis*. The concept is important enough to theologians that the kenosis is

a central organizing principle for those who seek to plumb the depths of the Incarnation. But what does it mean for the Son, who is God, to empty himself? This passage alone is not sufficient unequivocally to flesh out its full meaning, but taken in the context of Jesus' life, death and resurrection, the Church has clarified its meaning and central importance.

It is clear that the Church has protected the two qualities of Jesus—his divinity and his humanity. Throughout the ages there have been those who would stress one at the expense of the other. A balance must be maintained, however, for the reality and power of the Incarnation to be kept intact—the reality of Jesus' existence on earth and the power of that reality to save us. To do this any modicum of justice, we should quote from the Letter to the Hebrews:

> Since then we have a great high priest who has passed through the heavens, Jesus, the Son of God, let us hold fast our confession. For we have not a high priest who is unable to sympathize with our weaknesses, but one who in every respect has been tempted as we are, yet without sin. Let us then with confidence draw near to the throne of grace, that we may receive mercy and find grace to help in time of need. (Hebrews 4:14–16)

This is only one of many places in Scripture that asserts the fact that Jesus was, in his human form, just as we are, except without sin, implying that this fact is central to the whole concept of the Incarnation. (We will encounter this thought again when we explore the formula of the Council of Chalcedon.) This emptying or kenosis is simply the process of giving up access to those characteristics of God that are incompatible with being human. Note that I am being very careful here not to suggest that he did not have them, but that he freely "chose" (whatever that may mean for God to "choose") to be constrained by human limitations before he was conceived as a human being in the womb of Mary.

Some would say that he gave up some exalted honor due his place in the Godhead in order to come down from heaven and be with us. While this certainly is true, it says nothing about the form he took. In this line of thinking, Jesus gave up nothing of his divine characteristics, only the right to be recognized as what he was. Clearly this position would be important to one whose primary purpose was to defend Jesus' divinity. In a world where his divinity is under attack, it makes sense to grasp at anything and everything that affirms his divinity and to oppose anything and everything that appears to diminish it. The Church would agree that the divinity of Christ must be defended at all cost, yet it would also posit that one cannot throw out the baby with the bathwater. One cannot destroy the reality and power of the Incarnation in order to protect one nature at the expense of the other. They both must be protected and kept in balance.[10]

The alternative answer is that he emptied himself of all three "omnis." Some might say that this protects his humanity at the expense of his divinity, but for the kenosis to be meaningful, he had to give up something meaningful. Giving up an honor or a right is simply a figurative nod to the concept without any reality. In fact, the Church has at least

---

10   Even the word "balance" has subtle implications that may not quite capture what was going on, but sometimes we simplify in order to understand the basics.

implicitly asserted that in his humanity Jesus did not manifest any of the three characteristics. The key term here is "manifest." Whatever he did, he had to accomplish through his humanity. Scripture says that he was manifested in the flesh. In other words, he made himself known in his physical humanity.[11] Likewise, we can assert that Jesus emptied himself of all three "omnis." He didn't lose them; he just gave up access to them while he was in his earthly ministry.

Why does all this matter? We give the same response as the last chapter. If he is the same as we are in every way except for his lack of sin, then we cannot ascribe to him characteristics that would make him infinitely different from us—that would be completely antithetical to the whole reality and power of the Incarnation. Only if he was like us *in every way* except sin can we take him seriously as a model for our lives and the Savior who takes our humanity back into God.

---

11   There are many pointers, but here is the critical section in the *Catechism of the Catholic Church* (1997), Libreria Editrice Vaticana, pp. 116121.

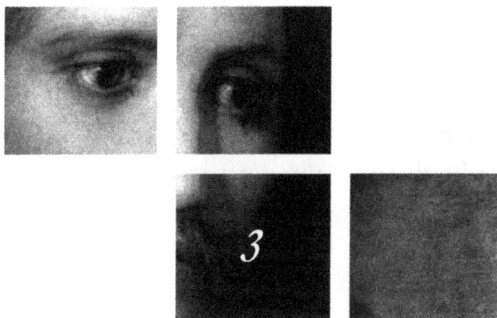

After the Resurrection

*After the resurrection and before the ascension, which of
these qualities did Jesus possess?*

The Death of Jesus on the Cross marks the end of the Incarnation as a completely human event. Jesus died a real
death, the same kind of death that our ancestors died and
the same kind that you and I will die some time in the future. Let us make no mistake about it—Jesus was dead. Why
do we need to make such a point of this? Let us consider the
way Charles Dickens writes about Marley, Scrooge's deceased
partner in *A Christmas Carol*. The story starts out with the
following:

> Marley was dead, to begin with. There is no
> doubt whatever about that. The register of his
> burial was signed by the clergyman, the clerk,
> the undertaker, and the chief mourner. And
> Scrooge's name was good upon 'Change for any-
> thing he chose to put his hand to. Old Marley

was as dead as a door-nail.

> There is no doubt that Marley was dead. This
> must be distinctly understood, or nothing won-
> derful can come of the story I am going to
> relate.[12]

The same might be said of Jesus. He was not in some transitory state, but all his bodily functions had ceased to work.
His heart had stopped, his brain activity had ceased, and his
organs had shut down. When he was laid in the tomb, he
was in exactly the same state millions of others have been in
when they were laid in their respective tombs. Just as Dickens asserts that nothing wonderful can come of the story if
we do not understand that Marley was indeed dead, is it not
all the more true of the death of Jesus, as this "story" is the
most wondrous story ever told? In fact, we could say that the
human death of Jesus is the crowning glory of the Incarnation. It is the punctuation of the salvific "statement" made by
the Son of God coming to earth to offer us the eternal life of
God. Clearly the resurrection and the ascension are essential
aspects of the Christ event, but they are tied inextricably to
the real death of Jesus on the Cross.

Once this fact is clearly etched on our brains, the resurrection seems all the more miraculous. How does God start
it all up again? Well, he doesn't exactly. The Jesus that is seen,
experienced, and even touched after the resurrection is not
precisely the same Jesus who was walking around a few days
before, at least not physically. He clearly is the same *person*,
but that person is now in a transitional state that has qualities
of both humanity and divinity. It is precisely because of this

12 J. B. Lippincott Company, 1976, p. 3.

transition, in fact, that Jesus participates in the three "omnis" in a different way. He now has access to powers that were not available to him before his resurrection. He now has access to knowledge that was not available to him before his resurrection. And clearly he is not constrained by place and time in the way that he was before the resurrection. Walking through doors was not a quality that he manifested before his death.

This transitional state only takes on real meaning if there is a real transition from one state to a state that is profoundly different. If all we are saying is that he exhibits his powers in a different way because he chooses to do so, then we do not have any real transition and the "story" loses much of its wonder, just as the ghost of Marley would lose much of his wonder if he were not seen as something essentially different from the Marley who was Scrooge's partner in life. The good news of the resurrection is that this same resurrection has been made available to us through Jesus Christ. Paul lays it out very succinctly:

> For if we have been united with him in a death
> like his, we shall certainly be united with him
> in a resurrection like his. (Romans 6:5)

Without his real humanity and his real death, his own resurrection loses its connection to us.

In the case of Jesus, he is neither a ghost nor merely an apparition. Scripture makes several points of placing him in a new state that even now we do not fully comprehend. Consider the following quotations:

That very day two of them were going to a

village named Emma'us, about seven miles from
Jerusalem, and talking with each other about
all these things that had happened. While they
were talking and discussing together, Jesus himself drew near and went with them. But their
eyes were kept from recognizing him. . . . So
he went in to stay with them. When he was at
table with them, he took the bread and blessed,
and broke it, and gave it to them. And their
eyes were opened and they recognized him; and
he vanished out of their sight. (Luke 24:13-15,
29-31)

As they were saying this, Jesus himself stood
among them. But they were startled and frightened, and supposed that they saw a spirit. And
he said to them, "Why are you troubled, and
why do questionings rise in your hearts? See
my hands and my feet, that it is I myself; handle
me, and see; for a spirit has not flesh and bones
as you see that I have." And while they still dis-
believed for joy, and wondered, he said to them,
"Have you anything here to eat?" They gave him
a piece of broiled fish, and he took it and ate before them. (Luke 24: 36-43)

He walked, talked, ate and could be touched, but he also
appeared, disappeared, walked through doors, and was not
readily recognized until something triggered that recognition. This was a new state that points us toward a new understanding of where our own resurrection takes us. But how
is it that someone in a transitory state can both eat and pass

through doors, both be touched by Thomas and vanish into thin air? The answer is, "I don't know." As a matter of fact, the sooner we get used to this answer as to *how* these things are accomplished, the sooner we start to access the mystery that has the power to transform us into new beings. Those who followed Jesus and experienced him in this state deeply believed that they had encountered their risen Lord, a belief that was foundational to their full understanding of the Christ event—the Incarnation. In fact, we should see this transitional state, not as Jesus leaving his humanity behind and regaining access to the characteristics of his divinity, but as taking his humanity with him as he returned to the Father. His glorified humanity becomes an instrument of his ability to be present not only to those in first century Palestine, but also to all of us throughout all ages.

Again, why does all this matter? Our understanding of the way in which Jesus participates in and accesses his divine characteristics is central to our understanding of and belief in Jesus—the one we call Son of God and Savior of the world. To carry around with us a sense of wonder of this intimate relationship between Jesus the man who is at the same time Jesus the Son, the second person of the Trinity, seated at the right hand of the Father, is to carry around with us an abiding faith that we are drawn into the life of God every moment of every day through the power of the Incarnation. To sit in wonder of the forty days that Jesus spent among his disciples after the resurrection and before his ascension is to sit in wonder of our own call to live fully into the gift of eternal life that has been offered to us through the power of the Incarnation.

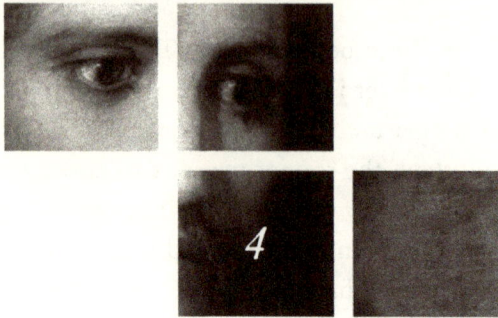

The Source of His Authority

In his earthly ministry, was Jesus the source of his own authority?

This subtle question points to the way Jesus saw his relationship to the Father. While certain statements in the Gospels seem to imply Jesus could act on his own accord and snap his fingers to get something done, other more explicit passages state clearly that Jesus saw his mission as living out the will of his Father. The following is such an example:

> "Don't you believe that I am in the Father, and
> that the Father is in me? The words I say to you
> I do not speak on my own authority. Rather,
> it is the Father, living in me, who is doing his
> work." (John 14:10)

While he certainly acted as if he were operating on his own authority, he clearly saw the source of his authority as the Father. In fact, the appearance that he was acting on an authority that did not come from the "powers-that-be" is precisely what frightened the temple aristocracy, who saw themselves as the only source of earthly authority regarding Judaism.

Therefore, just as a police officer exercises the authority delegated to him by the city of his employment or the president of the United States exercises the authority granted him by the Constitution of the United States, Jesus exercises the authority granted him by the Father, making the Father's authority his own. This is clearly a relationship particular to the emptied, incarnate Lord—the one who placed himself in a dependent relationship to his Father during his mission on earth.

Why would one be inclined to assert that Jesus acted on his own authority? Once again we can appreciate the desire to protect his divinity, and clearly the Son who sits at the right hand of the Father as the second person of the Trinity *is* the source of his own authority. To suggest that Jesus must look outside himself for authority implies some kind of reduced status. How can we hold Jesus up as the Lord and Savior of our lives and see him as anything less than God? And how can we see him as nothing less than God if we do not ascribe to him all the rights and privileges of God—including being his own authority? Good question!

The alternative answer would be to take him at his word and try to understand those more confusing passages in light of this dependent relationship that is implicit in the Incarnation. His words to Pilate, "Do you think that I cannot appeal to my Father, and he will at once send me more than twelve legions of angels?" (Matthew 26:53) might imply to some that he could simply snap his fingers and get done whatever he wanted. When a general snaps his fingers, he is operating on his own authority. When mom and dad snap their fingers, they are operating on their own authority. Jesus was , however, in a very special relationship to the Father during the Incarnation—a dependent relationship—and while it might look like he could simply snap his fingers and get done whatever he wanted, the orthodox understanding that takes the whole picture into account is quite different. Throughout the Incarnation, Jesus was in constant communion and communication with the Father, and the Father's will was the driving force of all that Jesus did. Thus we would say that the answer to this question is *no*, Jesus was not the source of his own authority while he was in his earthly ministry.

Why is this important for us as followers of Jesus? Simply put, the relationship we are called into with respect to God is one of total dependence. We are to see God as the ultimate authority in our lives. We are to be in constant communion and communication with God such that we can constantly discern his will and make it our own will. Sound familiar?

In other words, we are called to precisely the same relationship with the Father as Jesus had. He is the model for every aspect of our lives, including our relationship to God. While he was here on earth, he somehow had to give up some things and take on the relationship that he offers to us. The incarnate Son of God emptied himself to become as we are in order to model for us who we were created and *called back* to be. If we ascribe to Jesus a relationship in which it is impossible for us to participate, then he no longer becomes a model—in fact, we are left with *no* model. We would have no idea what this relationship should look like.[13]

---

13   From a Catholic perspective, it is interesting to note that even Mary would be lost without the model her son showed her for complete surrender to the will of the Father. The Incarnation could not take place, because (in

This dependent relationship modeled by Jesus and offered to us becomes central to our own salvation—our own access to life at its fullest.

some mystical eternal sense) Mary could not participate in the saving grace of the Son which gives her the capacity to offer an eternal *yes* to the will of God. In other words, the whole salvation event would be messed up if the incarnate Jesus were not in a dependent relationship to the Father. Not only would Mary be lost, but we would be lost as well.

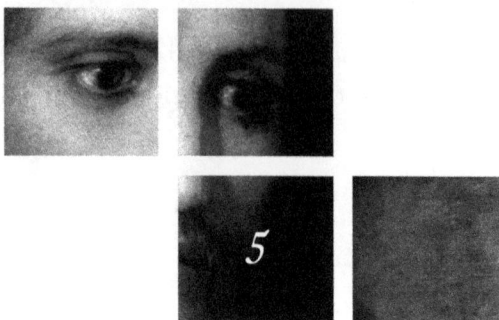

My Own Authority

As a Christian do you have any authority?
If so, what is the source of that authority?

Clearly Jesus expected us to exercise some form of authority after he was gone. The teaching given to the Apostles at the Last Supper pointed toward a ministry that could only be accomplished if they had been granted the authority to do it. Our question, however, is this: What is the source of that authority? Let's look for a moment at the nature of authority and the importance of its source.

If we look at one who has authority, such as a police officer, two aspects of authority are clear: (1) it is granted by some outside agency, and (2) it is exercised within some constraining jurisdiction. It is important to note that the outside source has itself been granted authority from some source outside itself, which gets its authority from some source outside itself, and so on. The policeman gets his or her authority from the city, which gets its authority from the state, which gets its authority from the nation, which gets its authority from the Constitution, which gets its authority from the people. Remember the Preamble:

> We the People of the United States, in order to form a more perfect union, establish justice, insure domestic tranquility, provide for the common defense, promote the general welfare, and secure the blessings of liberty to ourselves and our posterity, do ordain and establish this Constitution for the United States of America.

For a democracy, the highest authority is the *people*. You can't go any higher.

Thus, the granting agency creates the jurisdiction by the inherent limitations of its granting authority. In other words, the city cannot authorize a policeman to operate outside the city. A state trooper cannot operate in another state.

What about Jesus? Jesus receives his authority from the Father and thus becomes an agent who has authority in the jurisdiction of God, which happens to be over everything everywhere, throughout all time. Jesus, therefore, has eternal authority; but what about us? There are clear passages that indicate that Jesus has passed along his own authority to us. Consider the following:

> "Peace be with you. As the Father has sent me, so I send you." When he had said this, he breathed on them and said to them, "Receive the Holy Spirit. If you forgive the sins of any, they are forgiven them; if you retain the sins of any, they are retained." (John 20:21–23)

This is a radical statement for a Jew who would have understood that only God can forgive sins. But if Jesus is God incarnate who has been given the authority of God the Father, and if he passes that authority along to those he leaves behind in the world to do his work, then we as human beings indeed have authority. It is the most broad-based authority possible that emanates from the highest authority possible—God—with the most far-reaching jurisdiction possible—all time and space. But this authority has some important qualifications that we will talk about in a minute.

First, we should ask, why might one be reluctant to claim such an authority? First of all, it is extremely bold to suggest Jesus has passed along his authority to us on earth. If we merely understand the role of Jesus as comforting us and telling us what not to do, then it might be hard for us to appropriate the radical authority and commensurate responsibility that he has granted us. We might also look at passages such as, "Judge not, that you be not judged" (Matthew 7:1) as an admonition to maintain a posture of submissive humility that may seem to be incompatible with the kind of authority Jesus demonstrated. When he was teaching the masses, or reprimanding the Pharisees, or running the moneychangers out of the temple area, he was clearly claiming an authority that was far beyond any earthly authority. This strikes at the heart of the problem the Jewish ruling class had with him—he was claiming an authority that was far above their own earthly authority, which they thought was as high as it got.

Another problem might be one's understanding of how to exercise the authority given to us through Jesus Christ. It is one thing to think of the authority in abstract and theological terms, yet it is quite another to see explicitly how it might be acted out. Do we put folks in jail? Do we run them out of town? Or do we simply sneer at them and refuse to sit next to them or share our ice cream with them? What do we do to exercise the authority given to us? This is not a trivial question. The Catholic Church, for example, has settled on a number of ways: canon law that prescribes rules and consequences not unlike civil law, [14] sacraments that bestow on followers certain standing in the Church, and of course, ultimately excommunication that relegates one who is deemed to be particularly recalcitrant to the "outer darkness."[15] Likewise, many Protestant churches exercise similar kinds of authority through their own codes of discipline and resort to ultimate consequences that effectively result in a kind of banishment. In the context of the sacraments, the idea that the Church has the authority to forgive sins through the Catholic sacrament of Reconciliation or through a more general form of confession and forgiveness is also a bit audacious. By whose authority does the Church do all this? It is therefore not too difficult to see that, if the Jewish aristocracy had trouble with the authority of Jesus, many today may have similar trouble with any authority Jesus might confer upon his followers.

What is the alternative, then? The alternative looks a lot

---

14   Recall that the Roman Church grew out of the context of Roman law. The inclination to codify came instinctively from the environment in which the western Church developed. The Eastern Orthodox branch developed in a context that stressed less concrete spiritual forms of governance. See *Code of Canon Law*, Canon Law Society of America, 1983, 751 pp. Many Protestant churches find their governance principles closely tied to Scripture.

15   Actually, the particulars of excommunication are a bit more subtle. To be in communion with the Church means that one can participate in the sacraments, particularly the Eucharist. Excommunication does not mean that one has been "driven off" but merely refused the sacraments. Many would find the distinction obscure.

like Jesus looked to the Jewish aristocracy. Jesus believed—
and acted upon—the truth that he had been given all authority to act on behalf of the Father, and thereby to show the
world the human face of God. If we indeed believe Scripture
that Jesus has conferred on his followers a certain authority,
then we are called to act on that belief, no matter how audacious it may look to others. So the answer to the question
is *yes*, we have been given authority by Jesus Christ. Jesus
passed that authority on to the Apostles, who then passed it
on to their disciples. This process of "passing along" is one of
the differences of opinion between the Catholic and Protestant churches. But even within this context, all would agree
that there are some limits. It would only make sense that an
orderly passing along of authority would imply some constraints. Protestants have conventions, synods, and hierar-
chies of authority. Even at the parish level, there are parish
councils, boards of elders, or vestries that exercise authority. For Catholics, of course, that hierarchy is quite formal,
from the parish priest all the way up to the Pope. We can say,
however, that Jesus was not talking to everyone; he was talking to those he chose to carry on his work. Inasmuch as we
are followers of the teachings of the Apostles as passed down
to us through an understanding of Scripture, we are followers of Jesus Christ, and we participate in the authority that
was granted to the Apostles. But how do we express this authority? There are two fundamental dimensions to our authority: that exercised by the Church and that exercised by
individuals.

From a Catholic perspective, certain critical manifestations of authority have been adjudicated by the Church as
the agency of the Apostles into the future to continue the
work of Christ in an orderly fashion. Why is it important

that there be an agency? It is clear that order and continuity require some form of codified standards of behavior that must flow from a perceived sense of authority and must be passed down to future generations as a baseline of common understanding. One might think of it like the continuity of a democracy that has a Constitution (Scripture) and organs set up by that Constitution, such as a House of Representatives and a Senate (Church) that have the responsibility for creating continuity with the Constitution and the intent of the Founding Fathers who were representing the people. Jesus, representing the will of the Father, established the Church as the organ of continuity that has both the authority and the responsibility for assuring that future activity is consistent with the will of God. Without the Constitution, we have political anarchy. Without the Church, (the Church would assert) we have a kind of religious anarchy that results in everyone for himself—splinter groups, charismatic leaders, a vast diversity of belief and understanding.

On the other hand, Jesus has called each individual to conform to the model that he has set forth in himself. There have always been individuals who "bucked" the Church: Galileo, Teresa of Avila, St. Maximus the Confessor, and Martin Luther, for example. As a result of the tensions produced by these followers of Jesus, the Church has changed—not always easily or quickly—but eventually.[16] The Church's recent apology for its treatment of Galileo is a perfect example. Teresa left a powerful witness to a life of holiness, but she

---

16   Likewise, there have been many whose leadership has been rejected, thus taking us back to our old friend excommunication. This is what makes Luther so interesting. He was rejected by the Catholic Church but still had a huge influence on the future development of its theology and patterns of behavior.

did so in the face of considerable opposition. The story of St.
Maximus is a particularly compelling example of one person
who stood firm in the face of opposition only to be affirmed
some time after he died a martyr's death.[17] Finally, there is
no question that the Protestant Reformation, with Luther at
its center, had a profound effect on the Catholic Church. All
you have to do is read the *Catechism of the Catholic Church* to
see references to the "priesthood of the faithful"[18] and a renewed emphasis on Holy Scripture[19] to see the tip of a theological sea change that affected the Church in every quarter.

The trick for us as individuals is to appreciate that the authority and concomitant responsibility that has been offered
to us is tied to our acting out the will of God. Let us not un-
derestimate the difficulty presented here. We may think that
God is calling us to "get the rake," when he is, in fact, calling us to "bake the cake." Our authority, therefore, comes
from our right interpretation of the will of God, and that interpretation is intimately related to the state of our spiritual
journey into oneness with Christ. But at least we know what

---

17   There is a very touching transcript of his trial in the St. Maximus vol-
ume of the *Classics of Western Spirituality*. While he was supported by the
powers in Rome, he was opposed by the Patriarch of Constantinople and
the Emperor, Constans II. Together they were powerful enough to create
an immovable block to the Christology that Max was insisting on. Insisting
can often get one in trouble. Jesus insisted.

18   The Protestant concept of the "priesthood of all believers" is clearly
reflected in the Catholic Church's understanding of the "priesthood of the
faithful." *Catechism of the Catholic Church*, p. 895.

19   The Catholic Church's understanding of the place of Sacred Scripture
in the life of the Church is clearly laid out in the *Catechism of the Catholic
Church*, pp. 3037. The following quotation captures the essence: The Church
"forcefully and specifically exhorts all the Christian faithful . . . to learn 'the
surpassing knowledge of Jesus Christ,' by frequent reading of the divine
Scriptures. 'Ignorance of the Scriptures is ignorance of Christ.'"

the issue is. Perfect communion with God will yield a perfect understanding of his will, and a perfect understanding of his will gives one access to the same authority that Jesus exercised, which flowed directly from the will of the Father. In other words, if God wants something done through you and you are an obedient and faithful instrument of that desire, you are given not only the power but also the authority to do it. While Jesus had the authority to drive the moneychangers out of the temple, you or I might be given the mandate and the concomitant authority to run off the drug dealers from in front of the local school. (Please note that possessing the mandate and the authority does not necessarily mean that the drug dealers will not shoot you—but then look what happened to Jesus.)

So in precisely the same way that the dynamic relationship of the Son with the Father yielded a manifestation of the authority of the Father, our ongoing dynamic relationship with God has the same potential. We can say unequivocally that we *do* have authority as God, the source of that authority—through Christ—grants it. Let's face it, it is not easy to state exactly what is going on with a limited vocabulary, but we need to keep trying.

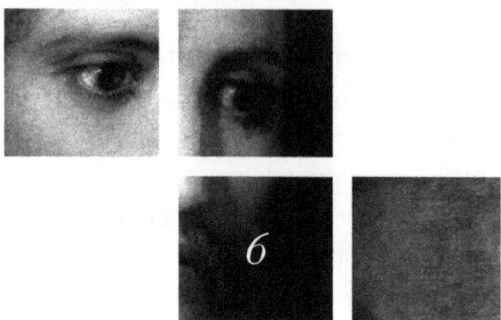

What Did He Know
and How Did He Know It?

Did Jesus know how to play golf?

In exploring this question we are directly addressing the knowledge of Jesus, only this time in a more concrete fashion. In this case we could say there are three issues that we need to address: (1) What did he know and how did he know it? (2) What can we know and how do we know it? (3) And finally, how do the answers to these questions inform our understanding of the Incarnation and its significance for us? To do this we will deal with a simple question of historical fact: the nature of the game of golf. If you or I were asked, "Do you know how to play golf?" we certainly would at least be able to say that it is a game played on a golf course with a little white ball and a bunch of sticks with heads on them that we use to strike the ball to try to get it into a hole in the ground in the fewest number of swats. What would Jesus have answered if he were asked that question? Our understanding of his response to this question will shed considerable light on our understanding of who Jesus was and how he related to those around him. Let's look at some possible responses.

The first is the common-sense answer; namely, there is no way Jesus knew how to play golf, because it had not been invented. The premise here is that Jesus had the same limits in knowledge you and I have. His capacity to know the future was based on an appreciation of the past and present and how these militate to direct the future. There are two possible reasons for believing that Jesus was thus limited: first, he was no different from any other human being and had no special claim on divinity, or second, his divinity manifested itself in ways that did not require a super-human knowledge. The first is of little consequence, since it is held by those who have difficulty with the whole idea of an Incarnation from the outset. These folks would be the first to say that they do not profess to be Christians and have little interest in all of this.[20] The second is a bit more interesting.

There was a time in the history of the Church when the idea of Jesus possessing unlimited knowledge was held in favor. Folks who believed that Jesus had limited knowledge were disdainfully called "ignorantists," in that they believed that the Son of God could be ignorant or lack knowledge of some things. Today we find a number of variations on this theme. Some would define ignorance narrowly as not knowing about *essential things*. If this more narrow definition of the word "ignorant" were accepted, the Church would have

---

20   Actually there may be some who do not profess to be Christians or even believe in God but *do* have some interest in "all of this." Now those folks should command our attention. They may actually understand more about some aspects of this than we do, who simply say we believe but have no understanding.

to say that Jesus could not have been ignorant about the essentials of his mission, the kingdom of God and other basic teachings that occupy the bulk of the New Testament. To suggest that he could have lacked knowledge in these areas would be tantamount to pitching out the whole salvation event. However, to most folks the general meaning of the word "ignorant" means a simple lack of knowledge of some specific thing. If I am a chemist, it is likely that I am ignorant of behavioral psychology. I am not stupid; I am just ignorant. It is OK for a child of seven to be ignorant of algebra, because he or she has not had it in school and probably does not have the intellectual capacity for it anyway. He is not stupid, merely ignorant. This is an important distinction we often make when discussing one's intellectual development.

We can certainly assume that Jesus was smart enough to grasp things that most of us would not have grasped without considerable guidance. On the other hand, we do not need to ascribe to him any extraordinary intelligence for him to be in prayerful ongoing communion with the Father. The Father had enough "intelligence" to go around.

For now, let's move on to the alternative, that Jesus did indeed know what golf was. The fundamental basis for this belief is that he was endowed with a special knowledge by virtue of his Sonship—the fact that he was God. One has a hard time justifying that Jesus was God and at the same time was ignorant of simple facts regarding the future. Certainly this difficulty makes a lot of sense, and one can see why many would simply assume he would have known not only about golf, but also about other events and aspects of the future. It is only when one gets specific and makes a list as we did when discussing his omniscience (which of course is the very same issue) that we start to get a bit uneasy and suspicious of this attitude. When we start such a list of things Jesus would have known, including the internet, the atomic bomb, the speed of light, relativity theory, how many atoms are in the universe and what time I will fall asleep on November 23, 2013, to 400 decimal places—we start to wonder if it makes any sense to ascribe to Jesus such an extreme amount of knowledge.

One of the difficulties of this latter position is something called the *beatific vision*. Many respected theologians in the Church, since at least Thomas Aquinas in the 13th century, have held that Jesus possessed a direct vision of God—the kind of vision that we will have in heaven:

> For now we see through a glass, darkly; but then
> face to face: now I know in part; but then shall
> I know even as also I am known. (1 Corinthians
> 13:12)[21]

This assertion by Paul of our state in heaven makes it clear that our knowledge will be vastly different than it is here. Now things are foggy and unclear. Then they will be crystal clear. Here we know God through his word, both written and living—Holy Scripture and most particularly the Son—and the activity of the Holy Spirit who brings us knowledge and understanding of God. In heaven we will see God face to face, and our knowledge will be at least as direct as it is of our parents and friends here, maybe much clearer. The basis for the assertion that Jesus possessed this kind of vision of God in his earthly ministry is the attitude, "How could it be

---

21 King James Version—The RSV translation is: "For now we see in a mirror dimly, but then face to face. Now I know in part; then I shall understand fully, even as I have been fully understood."

otherwise for the Son of God?"[22]

What is really interesting about this concept is that there is a wide range of interpretations about what exactly we mean by the beatific vision. If we define the beatific vision as the way we will see God face to face in heaven, then some would say Jesus continually rested in the beatific vision, continually experiencing that state of ecstatic union with the Father. [23] Others might say the beatific vision simply gave Jesus access to fundamental truths that emanate from the Father in

---

22   Two contemporary Catholic theologians are Karl Rahner (*Sacramentum Mundi*, v.1, pp. 151_153) and Bernard Lonergan (*Early Works on Theological Method I, The Collected Works of Bernard Lonergan*, 2010, University of Toronto Press, p. 420).

23   This might need some further explanation. Here is a quotation from the Catholic Encyclopedia of 1910—"The basis for the privilege of the beatific vision [seeing God face-to-face as we will in heaven] enjoyed by the human soul of Christ is its Hypostatic Union with the Word. This union implies a plenitude of grace and of gifts in both intellect and will. Such a fullness does not exist without the beatific vision. Again, by virtue of the Hypostatic Union the human nature of Christ is assumed into a unity of Divine person; it does not appear how such a soul could at the same time remain, like ordinary human beings, destitute of the vision of God to which they hope to attain only after their stay on earth is over. Once more, by virtue of the Hypostatic Union, Jesus, even as man, was the natural son of God, not a merely adoptive child; now, it would not be right to debar a deserving son from seeing the face of his father, an incongruity that would have taken place in the case of Christ, if His soul had been bereft of the beatific vision. And all these reasons show that the human soul of Christ must have seen God face to face from the very first moment of its creation."—I would just say this unequivocally: the bold typed "reasons" fail to take into consideration the fact that the Incarnation is precisely how it is possible for the divine Son to relate to the Father *without* the beatific vision as defined here. In fact, through the Incarnation Jesus *was* in some profound sense "an ordinary human being," while at the same time being the eternal Son of God. There is much to chew on.

such a way that he saw those truths clearly and could not have erred in areas of essential truth regarding his mission. Still others deny the beatific vision altogether by asking the question, "How could one who is in direct contact with the brilliant light and life of God suffer and struggle and question?" One might ask more simply, "How does one peel potatoes with the full light of God shining in one's eyes?" One option might be to suggest that certainly the gift of the beatific vision was granted to Jesus at certain places and times at the discretion of the Father.[24] Many theologians who are reluctant to dismiss such an historically established concept would say the beatific vision is that intimate, uninterrupted relationship between the Son and the Father. If it is taken in this sense, few would deny that Jesus possessed this throughout his earthly life.

To lay out all the pros and cons of this most arcane of issues, which, by the way, has never been explicitly settled by the Church, would be far beyond the scope of this little work and probably the ability of its author. Let us just say this: there is nothing in official Church teaching that requires a specific interpretation of the beatific vision. Consequently there is much in orthodox teaching that is perfectly at home with the concept that Jesus had limitations to his knowledge. Thus, one could say unequivocally that a perfectly orthodox answer as to whether Jesus knew how to play golf is *no*, it had not been invented. While he knew what he needed to know to accomplish his mission, there is no compelling reason to ascribe to him any additional extraordinary knowledge that would fall outside the normal limits of human intellectual capacity. This answer fortifies his humanity and, as we will

---

24   This *discretion* will be revisited as we work our way through the miracles of Jesus.

see, does no damage to his divinity.

Let me mention here a point on methodology. Everyone who is interested in understanding more about Jesus in theological discourse must learn to examine words. When addressing any question that is composed of *words*, and it is hard to image one that is not, since we appear to think in terms of words, one must always ask, "What do you mean by...?" In this particular case, it would be wholly appropriate to ask, "What do you mean by the word *know*?" or "What do you mean by the words *beatific vision*?" What we usually find is that the source of our disagreement, if we have one, is in our understanding of the definitions of the words we are using. An atheist has a definition of God that he or she does not believe in. You or I may have a definition of God that we *do* believe in. What we might very well find is that I too do not believe in the God as defined by the atheist, and just possibly, with a little work and generosity, the atheist might just believe in the God as defined by me, or, even better, the Church, if I avoid the use of the word "God." The discussion regarding the beatific vision is a particularly good example, because the definition of the term is very deep and requires a host of subsidiary terms, the definitions of which may themselves be murky. The challenge posed in *The Quiz* is to take the most generally accepted definitions of the terms being used and try to ask in what way they apply to the most generally accepted understanding of Jesus. In other words, it behooves us to *keep it simple.*

So what does all this mean for us? Our limited human capacity to know and understand is completely sufficient for us to live fully into the eternal life of God that Jesus showed us. If Jesus had demonstrated some completely alien form of intelligence, we would be forced to say that the life of God as

Jesus lived it was inaccessible to us. This might be a total betrayal of the Incarnation. It might be like trying to catch a bus flying by at sixty miles an hour. Good luck! The bus has to stop for us to get on, and the Son has to "slow down" for us to get on the path to the life we are intended to live.

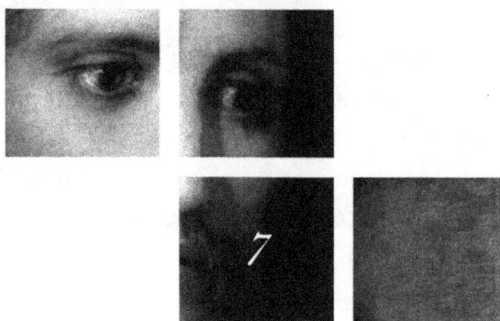

Play the Game

If Jesus had known how to play golf, could he have made a hole-in-one whenever he wanted to?

Now that we have seen just how tricky some of these seemingly simple questions can be, let us move on to another that is a huge trap for many who think of themselves as committed Christians. Here we are challenged to think about what we mean by the phase, "whenever he wanted to." We all know what a hole-in-one is. We also know that an extraordinarily skilled professional golfer—one who has had years and years of practice—hits a hole-in-one only rarely. Why would we expect someone who never practiced to be able to make one at will? If it were so, we would have to attribute that ability to something other than normal human ability. That does not mean it could not be attributed to Jesus as the divine Son of God, but at least we are duly warned of the trap (one might call it a bunker) that is lying out in the spiritual and intellectual fairway.

We have previously asserted that Jesus was not omnipotent

in his humanity, and his humanity is the only tool he had to work with. It is not that he did not possess the divinity ascribed to him, but that some of its characteristics were made unavailable to him on a day-to-day basis. We might say they were put into escrow or "blind trust." We also assert that Jesus did indeed perform miracles such as the changing of water into wine. If he could have done that, certainly a hole-in-one would have been much more within his grasp. Since others have done it, why wouldn't we assume Jesus could do it?

The most obvious answer for a Christian who sees Jesus as God incarnate, and one therefore given most often is, "Well, I guess he could have, if he had wanted to." What this answer does for us is to preserve our perception of his divine powers—and thus his divinity—while ostensibly allowing him to function like the rest of us. We modern Christians tend to start with Jesus' divinity and then struggle with his humanity. Recall, however, that the Apostles assumed his humanity and had to struggle with his divinity. The challenge here is to understand the implications of the phrase, "whenever he wanted to." We are asking about the nature of his will and desire while playing a game and his ability to achieve that desire. We will develop these thoughts in a bit.

The alternative is simply to assume that he could not have made a hole-in-one whenever he wanted to because no other human being has that kind of power. Again there are two reasons why some might take this position: first, they do not believe in the divinity of Jesus, and second, they require a full humanity for the Incarnation to work. As before, we can discount the first situation as the right answer for the wrong reason. The second reason is more challenging, and this is what we will try to clarify.

Here is the puzzle. It is not the "whether" but the "when" and the "how" that challenges us. If we were to understand under what circumstances Jesus turned water into wine, we would pretty much have our answer concerning his ability to make a hole-in-one. Let us clarify the "whenever he wanted to." Here we are talking about the relationship of desire and will to successful action. If we assume that Jesus could have played games, then we must assume that he would have played with integrity, since he could do nothing else. Maybe some would think that this assumption is a stretch, but a close look at the body of knowledge regarding the life of Jesus would militate in favor of a man who operated with perfect integrity. In other words, his thoughts and actions were perfectly in tune with each other. And as Christians, we would assert that they were not only in tune with each other, which is one level of integrity, but they were perfectly in tune with the will of the Father, which is the ultimate level of integrity.

So, if he is playing at all, he is giving his best, because that is the contract that all players have with each other. You might think naively that we don't have to play to win and that especially the man of love would not have wanted to make us feel bad by beating us at golf or tennis, or darts or the hundred-yard dash. Let me give you an example that I hope might clarify this issue. I used to play squash with a precious friend, Roger. One day we were playing "hot and heavy," and he got ahead. I then noticed that he was not playing as hard as he had been. I challenged him to explain. He said that he did not like to win, at which point I asserted unequivocally that if he was not going to try his best, I was not going to play with him. That was the last game we ever played. I felt that we had an implicit contract with each other, and as long as that contract was being upheld, we had a legitimate, authentic game—one that had integrity. Neither of us was acting. We were giving our best. The fallacy of his position, I felt, was that he did not like to win because he could not stand the notion of making me feel bad by making me lose. In his eyes, this was kindness, and I have known few people as kind as Roger. What he did not realize was that I reveled in a good game, and it did not matter one tiny bit who won. Winning or losing were incidental consequences of a good game. I could have had as much fun losing to well-executed shots by my opponent as I could by winning as a result of my own well-executed shots, and I expected the same indifference from Roger. I am telling you this because I have to believe that Jesus would have played any game with great gusto, having no care who won and expecting those with whom he was playing to have the same attitude. The only thing that would have made him angry would have been someone's ego getting in the way of the purity of the game—someone focused only on *winning*. He would not have played if doing so would have distorted one's integrity—one's relationship with God.

Let us return to the question at hand. What is it that each golfer tries to do? Put the ball in the hole in the least number of stokes, which would be a hole-in-one on each hole. Thus, if Jesus were playing with integrity, he would have wanted the ball to go in the hole every time he struck the ball. Here is the dilemma: if he wanted the ball to go in the hole, and he had the power to do so, it would go in the hole. This is where the statement, "Well, I guess he could, if he wanted to," falls apart. We can't have Jesus operate with integrity and at the same time not want the ball to go in the hole, so we believe that if he *could*, then he *would*. We are left

with only two legitimate answers: *yes* or *no*. Either he had
the powers that go far beyond those of any normal human
being and the answer is *yes*, or he was limited as we are and
the answer is *no*. How does our understanding of the Incarnation help us to sort this out? We are still confronted with
the miracles that clearly were a demonstration of powers that
stretched beyond normal human capabilities. How could one
who could change water into wine be limited on the golf
course? Can you imagine Jesus whacking the ball into the
woods or into a water hazard? How can we understand Jesus'
relationship to the Father during the Incarnation in a way
that will help us clarify this problem?

First, there is one concept concerning Jesus that must be
operative for the Incarnation to be legitimate. One of the
most powerful concepts in all of Paul's letters is the following:

> And being found in human form he humbled
> himself and became obedient unto death, even
> death on a cross. (Philippians 2:8)

The concept of *obedience* is deeply significant. One is obedient to someone other than oneself. Obedience requires a
surrendering of will, a yielding of self-interest. As we discussed above, if Jesus was operating with integrity and he
was obedient, his obedience to the will of the Father must
have been real. In other words, for something to happen in
the life of Jesus, we would assert that it was in accord with
the will of the Father and that Jesus was the obedient instrument of that will. In this case, how would we understand
that Jesus could play a game of any sort, legitimately want
to do his best, and see his effort in the context of the will of
the Father? Here is a proposed solution to the dilemma. If

the Father wanted the water turned into wine, and the Son was the willing instrument of the Father's will, the water became wine, not just cheap wine, but the best wine. If the Father wanted the Son to make the blind see, and Jesus was the willing instrument of the Father's will, the blind saw. But most of the time the Father's will was for Jesus to "play the game." This is crucial. Play the Game! In other words, enter into the life of your fellow man, and play the game as they have to play it in order to understand their problems, pain, joy, and temptations.

> For we have not a high priest who is unable to
> sympathize with our weaknesses, but one who
> in every respect has been tempted as we are, yet
> without sin. (Hebrews 4:15)

So if the Father's will for the Son most of the time was to "play the game," then not only could he not make a hole-in-one whenever he wanted to (which would have been all the time he was playing golf, because that is what golfers want—*all the time!*) but he could not even hit the green, if he hadn't practiced. To see this any other way may be to distort the Incarnation to the point of irrelevance.

But here is the other side of the coin. If the Father wanted the ball to go into the hole through his incarnate Son and the Son was the obedient instrument of the Father's will—*the ball would go in the hole.* All of the miracles Jesus performed were predicated on the authority and will of the Father. In the Incarnation, Jesus took on a relationship to the Father that was one of *obedient Son.*

So why does it matter? Who cares whether Jesus could make a hole-in-one or not? To the degree we can relate to the life of Christ, to the degree his life is like our lives, is precisely the degree to which we can yield to the possibility of being like him. We might take it further and consider the possibility of being transformed into his *perfect likeness—right now.* The whole point of the Son dwelling with us in order to reunite us with God is based on his simultaneous intimate relationship to the Father and to us. When we create artificial barriers in terms of extraordinary powers, we separate ourselves from Jesus and Jesus from us and destroy the power and efficacy of the Incarnation to change us into all we are intended to be.

Perfection

Name one human being who was perfect
in the eyes of the Father.
Do you consider Jesus to have been perfect?

Ah, perfection—what a trap! These two questions, as you will see, are really addressing the same issue. Again (and always) we must consider what we mean by the words *human being* and the word *perfect*. Although most of us think we know what we are talking about when we use the term *human being*, as you will see, it behooves us to be careful how we define it. We will say that a human being is an individual who exists in the temporal world (that is the earthly world of you and me) and functions through an integrated set of human characteristics. The word *perfect* is much more challenging. There are at least four broad perspectives from which to view our understanding of perfection: Greek, Latin, Old Testament Hebrew and New Testament Christian. Each of these has elements of the other but puts a little different spin on the concept. We find some valuable morsels in these spins that we can use in answering the questions posed.

The Greek concept of perfection, as represented by the teachings of Plato, relates to a comparison to some ideal. This ideal is represented by the "archetype" that exists in the mind of God. An example of this understanding would be the ideal or perfect circle. All earthly circles are merely approximations to the archetype. This understanding is conjured up in most of our minds when we use the term *perfect*. Something perfect is judged to be thus relative to an outside ideal. Here is the rub: from whose perspective is it perfect—mine, yours, your mother's, your spouse's, your neighbor's, the police's, the EPA's, the Vatican's, God's? Many wince at the very concept of perfection, because it implies just one more intolerable burden placed on us by some outside agency. And indeed that might be a proper attitude, if the agency is of this world. Unfortunately that is precisely the way we usually consider the idea of perfection. A "perfectionist" is trying to live up to some ideal that often is self-defined and self-imposed. Even worse is a set of ideals established by a boss, parent, or teacher. That is why perfectionism often is considered to be a neurosis or a form of compulsive behavior. In any case, it is not considered to be healthy.

Aristotle, also considered to be of the Greek school of thought, considered the term *perfect* to have three aspects: (1) complete, (2) the best, and (3) that which best fulfills its purpose. Here we can see the same kinds of difficulties. Who defines when something or someone is complete? The best relative to what? The purpose defined by whom? We still end up with what appears to be some form of absolute reference point to which we are making a comparison. We do seem, however, to be honing in on the idea that all the pieces of the puzzle work together for their proper end. In other words, all the parts are integrated and we are operating with *integrity*.

The Latin understanding is derived from the Greek and is best expressed by St. Thomas Aquinas. He makes a distinction between that which is perfect in itself (e.g. God[25]) and that which is perfect in satisfying its purpose.[26] In the first case we see the idea that perfection is something intrinsic to one's very being. In the second case we see some external reference which must be defined.

If we compare some references to perfection from an Old Testament Hebrew point of view to those found in the New Testament, we start to get a deeper understanding of what kind of perfection we are talking about. We must consider the Hebrew word that we translate as "perfect." In Leviticus 11:44 God directs the people of Israel to "be holy [set apart, sanctified, separated], for I am holy." Here is a clear parallel of the statement of Jesus in the New Testament, "You therefore, must be perfect, as your heavenly Father is perfect" (Matthew 5:48). Thus, we could say without much of a stretch that to be perfect is to be holy. Later in Leviticus God requires the Hebrew sacrifice to be *perfect*; "there shall be *no blemish* in it" (22:21). In the New Testament, Paul admonishes the followers of Jesus to be "blameless and innocent, children of God *without blemish* in the midst of a crooked and perverse generation" (Philippians 2:15). Here the parallel to a sacrifice without defect is powerful. In Psalm 18:30 the psalmist says, "This God—his way is perfect." In the New Testament we find in the first letter of John the statement, "No man has ever seen God; if we love one another, God abides in us and his love is perfected in us" (4:12). These references to a "way"

---

25 *Summa Theologica*, First Part, Q4
26 *Summa Theologica*, Part 1 of Second Part, Q55, Article 1, "I answer that."

and a process of being "perfected" both imply that perfection is not only a static ideal but also a pathway.

From all of these quotations we might draw some conclusions. Perfection for Christians is found in God. God is the source of any external yardstick of perfection. To ask the question about anyone's perfection is to ask the question concerning the degree to which one can share in the perfection of God as an ideal as well as the degree to which one moves along a pathway prescribed by God—a state of being as well as a movement toward a purpose or goal. We could, therefore, state that the proper Christian understanding of perfection is living fully into the will of God for us—not only an ideal for our state of being right now, but also a process of making our way to the goal that God intends for us. In other words, the proper understanding of the idea of personal perfection is "that which we were created to be." Another way of saying this is to be living in perfect integrity where all the pieces of our being—our minds, our hearts, our actions, our thoughts, our desires, our fears—are in line with the best we can be, relative to the will of God for us. With this in mind, let us look at some possible answers.

To answer the first question, one might be obliged to look beyond Jesus, because one does not consider him to have been a true human being. Let us first deal with the concept of human being as it applies to Jesus. The Council of Chalcedon tried about as hard as one could to clarify this issue and yet still gave some wiggle room that gives us trouble even today. Jesus was described as having both a human and a divine nature but was considered to be only a divine *person*. In the Chalcedonian sense, the word "person" takes on a very specific definition that is much deeper than simply an individual. Personhood was taken to be the very essence and the source of one's being. They thought it essential to ground Jesus in his divinity, even though he was manifest on earth in human form. Since Chalcedon talked about Jesus being a divine *person* with two natures, it is clear how some trained in theology would equate the term human *being* with human *person* and therefore shy away from this designation. It all depends on what we mean by the term "being." If we mean an integrated whole that functions through his humanity, then Jesus clearly falls into this category. He was fully human in every way and yet without sin. And sin does not define humanity. All we may be able to do is look at how the term is used and whether it has been applied to Jesus. The one quotation that comes to mind is from Pope Benedict XVI as follows:

> The Logos so humbles himself that he adopts a
> man's will as his own and addresses the Father
> with the I of this human being[27]

Clearly the Pope of the Catholic Church, an accomplished theologian, knows of the subtle distinctions at stake by the words he uses to describe Jesus. So we will use the words "human being" as a way of asserting Jesus' full humanity without diminishing his full divinity. It happens that what the Apostles saw before them was a man—a human being. If indeed we can say that Jesus was in the Incarnation a human being, then it would make sense to ask if we would consider him to have been perfect. If that were the case, we could then go on from there and ask if there were others. Now let

---

27 Ratzinger, Joseph, 1986, *Behold the Pierced One*, Ignatius Press, p 41. Note that his use of the word "adopts" in no way implies the kind of "adoptionism" that has been rejected by the Church, by which Jesus during his lifetime was adopted by God as his Son as a result of an exemplary life.

us deal with the idea of perfection.

If we take Jesus to have been a human being, then we must consider our understanding of perfection and determine if Jesus fills the bill. First, we would certainly assert that as Christians we take Jesus as the model for our humanity. So in the sense of being an ideal, he certainly meets that test. If someone else were a better model, then *he or she* would be the highest and best. By definition then, Christians hold Jesus to be the one better than whom there is no other. If his purpose was to be the savior of the world, then Christians would say that he fully lived into his purpose. If integrity is a yardstick, we would say that Jesus shows us both kinds of integrity: one in which all the parts of his being work together and the highest form, one in which all the parts work in accord with the will of the Father. If holiness is our yardstick, then Jesus defines for us what it means to be holy. In other words, no matter how you wish to define perfection, Jesus is the model. Jesus is, thus, the model of human perfection.

But there is another twist, if you happen to be Catholic (or Eastern Orthodox or Anglo-Catholic). Number two on the list is *Mary*. Why is this important? Because Mary, while a *human being* just like her son, was also a human *person* in a Chalcedonian sense. She was fully and only of the human order. She did not have a divine nature like her son except inasmuch as she participated in that nature through her communion with him by the grace of God. So it is perfectly clear that, if Mary was without sin, as has been proclaimed by the Church, then we have another model of human perfection. If we have answered the question regarding the way in which Jesus is the model for our lives and solved any confusion regarding his divinity (if we truly understand the teachings of the Church), then we should have no excuse for confusion regarding Mary.

Here is another angle to this perfection idea. It is certainly true that the saints led exemplary lives. It is also true that they would have been the first to point out their shortcomings. How might we reconcile the possibility of perfection with our own perceptions? We must understand that we are not necessarily the best judges of our state of grace, holiness, or perfection. That is God's job. Certainly we know when we fall massively short, but it just may be that our struggle to do the will of God *is* in fact the will of God. Just as Jesus was called at times to *play the game*, we too are called to play the game, and the way we do it may be seen by God as his will for us and thus be seen as perfection. In other words, sometimes the way we play the game or enter into the process of life *is* the standard we are seeking. We use Jesus as a guide for fundamentals like love and truth, but ultimately we must decide on the way we are to live our unique lives. We make judgments about what we think is in accord with the way of love and truth, and we hope that we have judged wisely. Unfortunately, we are not in a position to know for sure. All we can do is keep paying attention, availing ourselves of every opportunity for sharing the love and truth of God, and have faith that God will see our lives as they really are and not as we perceive them. In other words, God is the only judge of our and other's perfection.

Of course the second question is just a different angle on the first. Consider the following piece of Scripture:

> For it was fitting that he, for whom and by
> whom all things exist, in bringing many sons to
> glory, should make the pioneer of their salvation
> perfect through suffering. (Hebrews 2:10)

While there are not a lot of places that speak directly about Jesus' perfection, there certainly are many that point us to perfection through him. The above quotation, at least as it has been translated in the RSV, points directly to his own perfection. We certainly can infer that precisely this perfection is the seed of our own inasmuch as we live our lives in accord with his.

One thing stated unequivocally is that Jesus was without sin:

> For we have not a high priest who is unable to sympathize with our weaknesses, but one who in every respect has been tempted as we are, yet without sin. (Hebrews 4:15)

> And being made perfect he became the source of eternal salvation to all who obey him. (Hebrews 5:9)

> Indeed, the law appoints men in their weakness as high priests, but the word of the oath, which came later than the law, appoints a Son who has been made perfect forever. (Hebrews 7:28)

We have said that something is perfect if it exists or acts in accord with some ideal and some purpose. Both of these are externally determined, but they are somehow intrinsic to the thing. For human beings we would say that the ideal is God and the purpose is the purpose for which we were created. It is clear that in this context Jesus is in "perfect" accord with both the ideal of God, since he is God in human flesh, and with the purpose that God had determined for him. He was in a broader sense in perfect accord with the will of the Father. To be in such a state of perfect accord is not to fall short of that will. The falling short is called sin, and so we can see the connection between Jesus' life in perfect accord with the will of the Father and the assertion that he was without sin. They are the same thing.

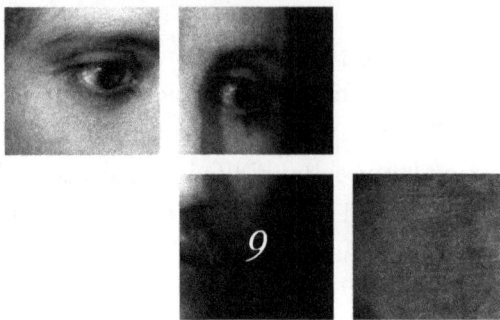

9

Our Own Perfection

*How much of Jesus' perfection has been offered
to us as humans?*

We have discussed the humanity of Jesus as well as the understanding that he was perfect in the eyes of God. This is not a stretch for those who believe that he *was* God incarnate. What helps us to understand how much perfection has been offered to us? What is the Scriptural basis for that understanding? What do we mean by our own personal perfection? What is the model for that perfection? How does the nature of the Incarnation inform our understanding? What is the difference between acting and being, and how does that difference deepen our understanding of our journey toward perfection? How is our perfection reflected in our relationships with others? What is the means by which we access that which has been offered to us? As you can see, this concept of our own human perfection is "loaded" and is intimately related to our understanding of the whole Christ event—the Incarnation.

As Christians, our understanding of our own call to perfection is driven by Scripture. Consider the following:

> You, therefore, must be perfect, as your heavenly Father is perfect. (Matthew 5:48)

> Jesus said to him, "If you would be perfect, go, sell what you possess and give to the poor, and you will have treasure in heaven; and come, follow me." (Matthew 19:21)

> And let steadfastness have its full effect, that you may be perfect and complete, lacking in nothing. (James 1:4)

These are clearly radical statements. To be perfect as God is perfect seems to be a completely unattainable ideal. There have been a number of attempts to interpret this concept in ways that make it more accessible. In other words, we might want to "water it down" a bit to make it more palatable. Some have said that the word "perfect" should be read "whole," with the assumption that wholeness is internal to us as individuals and perfection is imposed or measured from the outside. The problem arises when we have to deal with the phrase, "as your heavenly Father is perfect." If we are whole the way God is whole, we would be hard pressed to see this kind of wholeness as anything short of *perfect*. Some have said that the word "perfect" should be read "compassionate," as if compassion is something that comes from within and is not measured by some external yardstick. Again we run aground with the phrase "as your heavenly Father is perfect." We probably could make a case that if we were called to tie our shoes the way God ties his shoes (if God had shoes), we would not only tie our shoes perfectly, but we would be perfect in every other way, since God would tie his shoes with perfect integrity—no part of his being would not be in perfect accord with every other part of his being. We will see that this idea of integrity is "integral" (not to press the concept too much) to our understanding of perfection.

The second quotation not only asserts that perfection is something we should be working toward, but also indicates that what we do and how we think about our lives are central issues in understanding the possibility of our own perfection. Here we can introduce the concept of "attachment" to material things as an important facet of the pathway towards perfection. Nowhere does Scripture say that material things are bad. In fact, the Bible is replete with references that God shows his love for man through material blessings. Jesus, however, places these material blessings in a new context by suggesting that we must not see our own deepest wellbeing in terms of them. We must be willing to do without them. Here he is suggesting to the young man that he give up his material "blessings" in order to be perfect. We might surmise that he is saying this because he knows that this material wealth is indeed a stumbling block for the man, and that he is not willing to give it up—he is attached to it. As long as we are *willing* to give up our material wealth, we are not attached to it, and the way is clear for us to live the life God wants us to live. We are willing to do the will of God. Thus, being *willing* to do the *will* of God is an integral part of our understanding of perfection.

The third quotation explicitly relates the word "perfect" with the word "complete." Again we could assert that wholeness, completeness, and perfection are intimately related. But how can we understand perfection, something that appears to be measured from the outside, and completeness, something that appears to be measured from the inside, in such a way that they are intimately related? One of the fallacies of our normal understanding of Biblical perfection is that it is measured by a set of standards such as the Ten Commandments, which are external to us. We see perfection as something that others judge. If I am to be perfect, I must do what others expect of me: what my parents expect of me, what my boss expects of me, what my spouse expects of me, *what God expects of me*. Ugh! This is overwhelming. I would have to jump through hoops all the time, always trying to guess what other people expect of me and then scramble to fulfill those expectations. In this case, however, we are talking only about the last expectation—what God expects of me. Here is the rub. Since God is the creator of all things, he must have had something in mind when he created *me*. Thus, that thing that he "had in mind" (whatever that might mean for the great unfathomable God), is the backbone of our perfection. The first and foremost aspect of my own perfection has to do with the degree to which I live into that which I have been created to be. This is where *integrity* comes in. To live into who we were created to be is to live with complete integrity. All the parts—physical, psychological, and spiritual—of who we are and who we have been created to be work together without conflict. This is precisely what completeness and wholeness are. Nothing is missing, nothing is malfunctioning, and everything works as it was intended to work without breaking down. We can think of this concept more easily if we think of a computer that works "perfectly": it does what it is intended to do without failure. If someone asks how I like my new car, I could easily say that it is "perfect."

In other words, it does exactly what I intended it to do when I bought it, which was precisely what it was manufactured (created) to do. We can now understand that our perfection is not judged by others but by the way we live into who we were created to be and how we live into the will of God for us, with no attachments that get in the way of understanding and acting out that will. Only when we do this will we be whole or perfect.

It is all well and good to have some abstract understanding of perfection, but where do we see this perfection manifest in the flesh? We have seen above that in some way God is the model of our perfection. But where do we get our understanding of the way God would express his perfection as a human being? Of course it is Jesus. Scripture points us repeatedly toward Jesus as the model for our own lives. If God is the model for our own perfection and Jesus is the model for our lives, then a little conceptual "algebra" leads us to the conclusion that Jesus is the model for our own perfection.

> For those whom he foreknew he also predestined
> to be conformed to the image of his Son, in or-
> der that he might be the first-born among many
> brethren. (Romans 8:28)

> "For who has known the mind of the Lord so
> as to instruct him?" But we have the mind of
> Christ. (1 Corinthians 2:16)

In other words, if Jesus is considered to be perfect, then we can assume that the model for our own perfection is Jesus himself. But how much of that perfection has been offered to us? There are three possibilities: (1) some of it, (2) none of it, or (3) all of it. We might be tempted to answer that *some* but not all of Christ's perfection has been offered to us just to be on the safe side. *Some* can range all the way from slightly more than *none* to slightly less than *all*. Unfortunately, this position would be a *non sequitur* (does not follow), since one cannot trade in portions of perfection. Either you get all of it or you get none. We might say that we can get some of his goodness, kindness, courage, and so forth, but we cannot get *some* of his perfection. So if we want to stay "safe," we are left with only one answer, given this understanding of Jesus and perfection: namely, we get *none*. We are simply not intended to be "perfect" in this life. We will and must always fall short of God's will for us. We can never be completely like Jesus. If this is our position, then we must do some creative interpretation of the meaning of the pieces of Scripture that (at least in translation) point us directly toward perfection. As we saw above, this attempt to reduce the power of the call to perfection lacks certain logical underpinnings. Therefore, the idea that we get *none* would seem to belie all of the Scripture we have thus far considered. How can we be called to perfection with Jesus as our model of perfection, if we are not offered the possibility of participating in any of his own perfection? This simply makes no logical sense.

The alternative, then, is that we get all of it. How would we justify such a radical understanding of Jesus? In the Incarnation he emptied himself of access to the characteristics he possessed as God that were incompatible with the human condition in order to participate fully in our human lives. One of the most powerful statements of the purpose of the Incarnation was written in the eighth century by the theologian Maximus the Confessor. He is called a "confessor" of the faith, because he died as a result of a stand that he took

regarding Jesus' humanity, which many in the Church and
state objected to. Finally the Church as a whole tackled the
issue and repudiated his opponents, but not before he suf-
fered mutilation and death for his beliefs. His writings are
some of the most profound statements of Christian orthodoxy, and here is one of the most powerful:

> The sure hope of the deification of humanity is
> the Incarnation, which makes of man god in the
> same measure that God became man.[28]

God reached down through the incarnate Son and drew
us up to where the Son was himself. The point Maximus
makes is that Jesus offered all of himself to us as the Incarnate Lord, and we can access that gift to the extent we follow him and are transformed into his very likeness. Basically
it is as if he says, "Look at me and *be* me in the world. I give
all of myself to you." More specifically, he gives all that he
was when he was in his earthly ministry. We might think
it is extremely audacious for us even to begin to place ourselves on the same plane as the Christ, the Son of the living
God. Since for him "equality with God was not something
to be grasped" (Philippians 2:5), how much more should we
shy away from some kind of equality with Jesus? With this
attitude, it is no wonder most might recoil from the very
thought of being "perfect" like Jesus.

We might, however, get confused about what the perfection of Christ means. Does it mean that we would be able to
snap our fingers and change water into wine or raise grandma from the dead? Does it mean that we would have to

---

28   Palmer, G. E. H. et.al., ed., *The Philokalia*,1986, Faber and Faber, Inc.,
Winchester, MA, v. II, par. 62, p. 177.

know everything that he knew? Does it mean that we would have to be crucified? Our understanding of the perfection of Christ is directly dependent upon who we think he was in his earthly ministry, and that is precisely what *The Quiz* is all about. If we are to see Jesus as the model for our lives, our compelling challenge is to dig deeply into who he was—how he thought and prayed and acted in accord with the will of the Father. This movement toward perfection certainly depends on how one approaches his or her life as a follower of Jesus Christ, but at least we should know where we are going, even if we are not quite sure how to get there.

It is, however, impossible to understand this radical call to perfection without addressing the means by which this transformation into perfection takes place. How does it happen in the context of church services and prayer and our lives in the community of faith? The Christian way that has developed and been acted out over the last 2000 years contains many dimensions that relate directly to our spiritual journey. All of these dimensions relate to a kind of surrender to the will of God and an understanding that we are "saved" by the life, death and resurrection of Jesus Christ. The question we have been addressing here is "saved from what?" Many would say that we are being saved from a life after death in eternal damnation—the fires of hell—and few would disagree with the benefits of such a salvation. But we are unequivocally saying here that we should also ask the question, saved *for* what? Our salvation relates not only to what happens to us after we die, but also to what happens to us right here and now. What we are saying is that through the Christ event, we have been saved *for* a life through which the perfection of the Incarnate Lord shines through us to the rest of the world. Through sacraments, our beliefs in the meaning of Jesus Christ, and our lives of prayer and compassion, we are drawn into the life of Christ. Therefore, we can say unequivocally not only that Jesus is the model for our lives, but also that the "getting there" is made possible by Jesus himself. He is not only the *model* but also the *means*. While *The Quiz* is mainly about the Incarnation as an earthly event and our earthly goal of transformation, Jesus promises much more after we pass from this earthly life to the next life with God. Right now he offers us all that he *was*. In the next life he offers us all that he *is*. Both of these are made possible by his actions as Savior.

In addition, he sends the Holy Spirit as the means of our understanding and of our empowerment to be changed into new people.

> "But the Counselor, the Holy Spirit, whom the Father will send in my name, he will teach you all things, and bring to your remembrance all that I have said to you." (John 14:26)

> And when they had prayed, the place in which they were gathered together was shaken; and they were all filled with the Holy Spirit and spoke the word of God with boldness. (Acts 4:31)

The role of the Holy Spirit in our journey toward God is an easy stumbling point for many. We often pray to God through Christ and ask the Holy Spirit to inform our lives or to fill us in such a way that we are changed into new people. We ask God *to act*, but we ask the Holy Spirit *to fill*. These subtle distinctions may or may not help us to grow in our perfection, but it certainly is clear that that growth requires the infilling of the spirit of God—the Holy Spirit. Only through such an infilling is the radical transformation offered to us made possible. So we could say that the Son breaks the bonds that keep us from being who we were created to be, and he sends the Holy Spirit to fill us with the spirit of God that draws us on that journey. Again, Jesus not only becomes a model for our lives but also the means by which we access that model—by his act of salvation and by the sending of the Holy Spirit.

Now the word "be" is interesting in the admonition to "be perfect." If Jesus is our model, it is very easy to ask the question, "What would Jesus *do*?" WWJD is a well known acronym that has found its way onto bracelets and bumper stickers. It is not a bad starting point if one wants to pattern his or her life on that of Christ, but it is only a starting point. Here is a particularly compelling piece of Scripture:

> I appeal to you therefore, brethren, by the mercies of God, to present your bodies as a living sacrifice, holy and acceptable to God, which is your spiritual worship. Do not be conformed to this world but be transformed by the renewal of your mind, that you may prove what is the will of God, what is good and acceptable and perfect. (Romans 12:1–2)

The three concepts that jump out at us are the ideas of *transformation, minds,* and *perfection.* It is clear Paul takes for granted that we are called to be changed by the "renewal" not just of our actions but more especially of our *minds,* and that the goal of transformation is what is "good and acceptable [to God] and perfect [in the eyes of God]." This radical transformation is not pressed forward as something unusual or especially onerous but is a simple conclusion of the life of Christ, what we call the Incarnation, both as model and as means. This radical transformation is taken to be the most basic principle of the followers of Jesus Christ.

Therefore, the kind of transformation he calls us to—the one reflected by Max's understanding of the Incarnation—is a transformation of *being*. The philosophers would call this an "ontological" transformation. Paul points to this kind of transformation when he talks about taking on not merely the actions but the *mind* of Christ. Medieval scholars would have said in Latin, *"agere sequitur esse"*[29]—action follows being. So the radical transformation into the very likeness of Jesus Christ is a deep transformation which in turn gives us access to our own perfection. Indeed, to be transformed into the perfect likeness of Jesus Christ is to be transformed into the person we were created to be in terms of both the ideal of God and the purpose of God for our lives. While we don't exactly know how this purpose is laid out, we can probably rest assured that it is not as simple as a roadmap. We may need to allow the concept to be a mystery that conditions our approach to life without feeling compulsive about determining the exact details at every turn. Let us just be clear about one thing: Jesus' perfection, with all that that might mean, has been offered to us right here and now.

We can see this radical transformation as a taking on of

29　Aquinas, Thomas, *Summa Contra Gentiles*, Book 3, Chapter 69, Paragraph 17. The phrase is contained in the statement, "If action is consequent to being actual, it is unreasonable that the more perfect act be deprived of action." The Latin phrase, "agere sequitur ad esse in actu" has been shortened by philosophers and theologians to be, *"agere seqitur esse"*—action follows being.

those things that make us whole and a giving up of those things that destroy our wholeness. What are some things that we might want to take on or expand? Well, there really are only two: love and truth. Each of these would require its own book to elucidate the depth of its full meaning, but we must at least acknowledge that Jesus captures the essence of his humanity by showing us what authentic love is in the context of a life lived in profound truth. How we love ultimately must be modeled on how *he* loved, and we do that by receiving the love that he offered us by his life and death. The depth of this love is found on the Cross, and we ultimately are called to be willing to offer our own lives as completely as he did out of love for others. Many have done this: missionaries, martyrs for the faith, saints, doctors and nurses, soldiers, scientists and many average everyday folks who give of themselves selflessly for the good of others. To have the courage to love might also mean having the courage to be steadfast—constant in the face of opposition. The Hebrew word "chesed" captures the constancy that God exhibits in his love for us. Implicit in this constancy is the idea that love and truth are intimately conjoined. We could say that there is no authentic love outside the context of truth, and there is no truth outside the context of love. For example, many in the civil rights movement paid a high price for their convictions grounded in what they believed to be *true* about the condition of mankind and expressed in the *love* for those for whom they struggled. Thus, perfection is intimately related to the way we receive the love and truth of Christ and offer that to others. There is no meaningful transformation into the perfection of Christ without a transformation of the way we love. This transformation finds its headwaters in God's love for us as expressed in the life of Christ. Furthermore, the way we live into the truth finds its origin in God and its most profound expression in the Incarnation of Jesus Christ.

On the other hand, perfection, while made available to us, comes as a result of leaving behind things that get in the way of our transformation. We may associate some of these things with safety and comfort, some with satisfaction and pleasure. To move toward this kind of radical transformation, we must step out in faith into unknown territory, trusting that the result will be new life. The most profound example of this kind of trust is the Cross of Jesus Christ. Here we see one who was willing to offer all of himself freely, not only that we might be saved from a shabby excuse for a life without God, but also that he might move from his earthly incarnation back to his place at the right hand of the Father. We are looking at a profound trust that results in a complete obedience that ultimately results in a massive transformation. We could say that this model of trust, obedience, and transformation is precisely the model for our own passage from the life we are leading to the life we are intended to lead. Consider the following:

> Then Jesus told his disciples, "If any man would come after me, let him deny himself and take up his cross and follow me. For whoever would save his life will lose it, and whoever loses his life for my sake will find it." (Matthew 16:24–25)

There is, therefore, some fundamental linkage between the Cross and the transformation Jesus calls us into—between losing our life and finding it. This points to a willingness to trust to the extent that we can see trials, both small and large, with which we are confronted every day, as doorways into transformation. Our crosses are not bad things that happen to us that we accept grudgingly and therefore have no power to change us, but those things that, when accepted graciously, have the power to make us into new people. Say that you have been in an automobile accident and have lost the function of your right arm. You have a choice to make. You cannot change what has happened, but you certainly can change how you feel about it. You can be bitter and frustrated at your newly reduced physical capability, or you can find a way to accept this condition and use it to become a new person, one with greater patience and compassion. Christopher Reeve, the actor who played Superman, fell from the horse he was riding and was paralyzed from the neck down. I am sure everyone, including himself, saw this as a tremendous tragedy, one that could easily have left him bitter and incapacitated, both physically and psychologically. Remarkably, as he forged ahead to deal with his situation, he came to see it as a blessing that changed his whole life for the better. His life was richer and more full of wisdom, compassion, and love. Now *that* is a cross—a doorway that few of us would choose to enter, but that has the power to change us into new people. As we start to pay attention to the words of Jesus and begin to understand what he asks of us, we will be on the road to continual radical transformation toward the perfection that has been offered to us—a perfection characterized by our willingness to receive the love and truth of Christ and to pass it on to others. Often it is the crosses in our lives that allow us to focus on what is really important in life. Jesus points us in the right direction by his words and his life.

We would be right to say this search for perfection is not only difficult but quite a struggle. It is not easy. So why

bother? What is the bottom line here? Well, just ask the computer that works flawlessly or the car that has just been tuned
up. They work without failure or conflict. What happens if
we work without conflict? What happens to *us* if all the pieces of the puzzle work together as they are intended to? It is
called the "peace of God which surpasses all understanding"
(Philippians 4:7); it is a peace that washes away frustration
and fear, sadness and anxiety. It is a peace that leads to joy—a
joy that only God can give. All you have to do is read a little
about the saints to understand what this joy looks like. We
might often ask *how* they did what they did in the face of a
host of adversity. What kept them going? We might also ask
why they did it. The answer, of course, is that somewhere in
their life journey they tasted that peace and joy that can only
come from God. They trusted what others who had gone
before them had said about God and Christ, surrendering to
the possibility that life in Christ—what we are calling here
the life of perfection—was the only alternative in the face of
the worldly, material-laden, self-absorbed life they had been
leading. Peace and Joy: not just any peace or any joy, but the
peace of God and the joy of God.

Let us see if we can pull some of these threads together. Our very creation is an expression of the will of God
for us. Some are men, and some are women. Some are naturally musically inclined, and some are mathematically inclined. Some are naturally jovial and extroverted, and some
are naturally quiet, thoughtful, and introverted. Some are
called to be the instruments of commercial activity and some
are called to be managers. Some leaders and some followers. Some are called to be husbands and wives, and some are
called to celibate lives with a deeper spiritual focus. God sets
those things up, and we are simply challenged to discern how

to express those natural characteristics or callings in our lives. The key here is that we are called to take on those things that are compatible with that created order and to give up those things that conflict with it. In other words, we are called to grow in integrity. As we become less attached to anything, we become more and more supple in our movement toward the person we were created to be. As we receive our "crosses" as opportunities to grow, we, well, *grow*. This growth expresses itself in our capacity for love and in our courage to live fully into the truth that is revealed to us. Ultimately this perfection in Christ yields a peace that surpasses all understanding—a joy that only God can give.

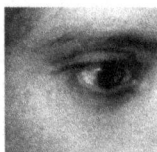

10

No!

Could Jesus have said "no" to the will of the Father? For example, could he have refused to go to the Cross?

The essence of this question hinges on one's concept of "free will." Freedom of choice has been at the top of the list of characteristics of God that were given to humanity when God created man in his own image and likeness. To commune with God requires a level of freedom to which God can relate intimately. For the relationship to be authentic, it must reflect a certain level of creativity, embodying the possibility of expressing something *new*. It must be alive and have the quality of *surprise*. The opposite would be like trying to relate to your vacuum cleaner. When I relate to my vacuum cleaner, I know how it will respond. When I flip the switch, it turns on, and when it turns on, it sucks up dirt. Nothing creative here! It might be ingenious, but not creative. When I relate to an opponent while playing soccer, I don't have any idea what he or she will do, but I know beyond a shadow of a doubt that it will be creative—usually at a level of creativity that I cannot match. This creativity, we might say, is a reflection of the very creativity of God as, well, creator. We therefore participate in the creative process by entering into creative relationships. We could even expand this idea to assert that God's creative impulse was shown in the stars and the planets, the sea and the dry land, the night and the day, but God's most stunning creation was mankind, created in the image and likeness of God for the express purpose of being in a creative relationship with God. In other words, mankind was created to be creative.

This creativity expresses itself through the choices we make. If we are an artist, it is reflected in the subject we choose, the lines we draw, the colors we use and the way we compose the painting. If we are an engineer, it is reflected in the problems we choose to tackle, the technologies we use, the size constraints we acknowledge, and the way we integrate the parts to make a whole. If we are a manager, it is reflected in the people we choose to work for us, the values we choose to adhere to, and the style of management we choose to apply to the problems with which we are confronted. And if we are a housewife or husband, it is reflected in the spouse we chose to be our helpmate, the way we structure our time, the way we order the living space, and the way we bring up our children. Thus, free will implies the ability and necessity to *choose*. As we will see, this capacity in no way stands in the way of a kind of strength of character that defines the choices we make, but it makes every choice authentic. The presence of a morally grounded "no" must have the legitimate possibility of a "yes" that may or may not be seen as a reasonable alternative, given the particular character traits of the person making the choice. In other words, an authentic "no" always implies the possibility of a "yes," and an authentic "yes" always implies the possibility of a "no."

Mary, the mother of Jesus, is an interesting example in this regard. While the nature of Jesus' responses to a number of situations could be seen as conditioned in a way that often confuses us regarding his use of free will, there seems to be little controversy concerning Mary. Her decision to say "yes" to the angel Gabriel resounds throughout history as a critical part of the Christ event. We hold up that surrender to the will of God as a central part of the Incarnation, for this "yes" set the stage for all that followed. In order for this "yes" to be authentic and meaningful, there is no question that the possibility of a "no" had to exist. What if she had not said, "Behold, I am the handmaid of the Lord; let it be to me according to your word" (Luke 1:38)? What if her response had been, "No way, I have a career!" Of course, it is conceivable that God could have used her in spite of her resistance, but that seems to be contrary to the way God works. She was chosen because she was already surrendered to the will of God. Her response was perfectly consistent with her character. The idea that she was without sin her whole life is just one way of asserting this posture to God's will, but there seems to be no question in her case that her "yes" had meaning only in the context of the possibility of her "no." Her "yes" was not the response of an automaton but the response of a human being who was utterly stunned by what was being asked of her. Her "yes," therefore, has profound meaning for us because it had profound meaning for her.

We should point out the connection between the word "meaning" and the word "context," both of which we have used to give thrust to our argument that a choice only is a *real* choice if there is a legitimate alternative. For something—anything—to have meaning, it must be in some form of relationship to something else. In other words, it must have a context. The wooden arm of a chair only has meaning as an arm inasmuch as it is related to the rest of the chair. Even if it is a broken piece, its' meaning as "arm" only means something if we know what an arm is in relationship to "leg" or "seat" or "back." The same is true for "yes" or "no." For someone to offer a "yes" without the context of a possible "no" robs the "yes" of context—of meaning. We would be hard pressed even to understand what we might "mean" in a specific circumstance by saying "yes" if the hearer did not either explicitly or implicitly understand something about the possibility of the opposite response. The way free will takes on powerful meaning is in the presence of disparate alternatives, the choice of which has implications or *meaning* for our life's journey.

The relationship between free will and creativity, surprise and choice, offers us the opportunity to see a rich context and meaning in which humanity acts out its gift of free will. When we are confronted by a choice, which we are just about every moment of every day—When should I roll out of bed? What will I eat for breakfast? How fast should I drive to work? What task shall I tackle first? When will I pack it in and go home? How will I greet my family (or my dog)?—we draw on an infinite number of possibilities. While we may often approach this banquet of possibilities as if in a fog, allowing our choices to be made more by habit or by others than by a deliberate desire for creativity and surprise, those possibilities are there staring us in the face nonetheless. As we mature and grow in our journey toward Christ, our appreciation of the banquet of choices becomes richer, and the possibility of extending ourselves into the world as a light for love and truth becomes greater.

Our understanding of free will not only informs our perception of human possibilities, it also informs our understanding of what it means for us to say that God has free will. To say that God responds to prayer and engages us in our own human history is tantamount to saying that God operates with these same characteristics of creativity and choice. While we act on this belief at least implicitly by our belief in God, we are forced to admit a fundamental lack of understanding of how this works. Does God's creativity look like ours? Does God make choices the way we do? The answer to these questions is unequivocally no, but, while we cannot understand how God operates, we can also assert that we believe that he does. This is all part of the mystery that is God, our approach to which forms the foundation of our posture toward life.

Here would be a good place to muse about God's omniscience and how we can enter into a creative relationship with God. One simple question might be whether God is ever surprised by my actions. It is all too easy to assume, since God knows everything, past, present and future, that God is never surprised. Certainly I am surprised by God—all the time. Sometimes I am surprised in a good way, as when I am overwhelmed by the kindness and gentleness of someone I encounter. Sometimes I am surprised by the abject frustration I encounter when I try to do something that clearly flies in the face of good judgment. Somehow I know that I have derailed—don't ask me how.

So it seems only fair that God might just be surprised by me once in a while—sometimes pleasantly surprised and sometimes disappointed, but surprised, nonetheless. My favorite story of surprise occurred when I was a senior chemistry major at a small liberal arts college, the University of the South, usually known as Sewanee. I had the distinction of being third in my graduating class in chemistry—*and last.* The two other chemistry majors went on to stellar careers in chemistry, and I went off to teach ninth grade physical science at a small prep school. Anyway, when I was called in to review the results of my comprehensive exam by the head of the chemistry department, Dr. Camp, I sat there with marked trepidation awaiting his austere pronouncement. He looked over the considerable stack of legal-sized yellow pages I had churned out, thought for a moment, and said in his inimitable high voice, "Uh, Mr. Fletcher—this is not too bad." I am sure I had exceeded his modest expectations, which would not have been hard to do, as I am sure they were very modest indeed. In other words, he was pleasantly surprised—as was I. It is hard for me to believe that God does not respond to me in the same way—with some level of gratification at the rare moments I rise above expectations.

On the other hand, I am compelled to relate a little story about my fourth grade teacher, Mrs. Summerall. She had been sick for a few days, and upon her return there was a considerable buzz of disappointment that she was back. She entered the classroom and said something that I don't recall, at which point I blurted out, feeling assured that she would appreciate my honesty and good will, that *they* were not pleased that she was back. Fully expecting that she would look at *them* with some kind of castigating glance, I sat quite satisfied with my newfound position of superiority. Instead Mrs. Summerall looked right at *me* and said, "Jonathan, I am surprised at you." Oops! I had miscalculated. It would not be the last time I would badly miscalculate my own response to different situations, but I hope that I have learned a little something from each one—maybe a big something from each one. I am not proud of those excruciating moments, but it is hard to believe that God does not respond to me in the same way—with disappointment in my shabby behavior.

Because the ability to be surprised is such a fundamental aspect of a creative relationship—a relationship that produces something new and possibly wondrous—I simply refuse to believe that God is not sometimes surprised by us, sometimes with a pleasant surprise and sometimes with a surprise of considerable disappointment. This statement has absolutely no theological basis, but is grounded on how the essential virtues of hope, trust, and love depend on free will and how free will results in a creative relationship. So let me make my most profound theological argument for how it is that God can be at the same time both omniscient and surprised. The answer is—*I don't know*! Sometimes the best answer to the paradoxes that continually pop up in our efforts to understand God is, "I don't know." If we ever get to the point that our complex theologies make us self-satisfied with our answers, we may have missed the most important aspect of God—that God is a mystery.

There is an entirely different discussion concerning the concept of free will. If free will is not just the ability to choose but related to a larger concept of "freedom," then we need to look briefly at how the nature of freedom can be understood. If the opposite of freedom is enslavement, then we must ask, what is it that enslaves us and deprives us of our freedom? The Church would unequivocally say that sin, the falling short of who we are created to be, captures us and constrains us in a series of ruts. For example, the sin of pride—thinking that I am the source of my own authority (at least that is one way of defining it)—distracts me from a larger truth that would open my life up to much greater possibilities. I am somehow trapped into a limited experience of what life has to offer. The sin of gluttony—yes, eating too much; I know that one well—limits me in a number of ways by my carrying around too much weight. I run more slowly, get winded too easily, and look fat in a bathing suit. Ugh! There, I said it. I may even die sooner than I would if I were not carrying around an extra 35 pounds. I am definitely trapped by the love of eating—tilapia étouffée, veggie-lover's pizza, cherry ice cream, oatmeal raisin cookies. I am free from a "choice" point of view to be enslaved from a "sin" point of view.

So what does this have to do with Jesus? We now have two issues to address: (1) did he have *free will* and how did that express itself, and (2) did he have the *freedom* that comes from being without sin and how did that express itself? There is no question that he had free will from both directions, so to speak. As man he had free will as a part of his humanity that was created "in the image of God" just like ours is. As God he gets free will from his very nature. But how did that express itself in the choices he had to make? Remember that he had the same choices that you and I have to make on a daily basis. Recall the list above and many more. One of our challenges is that the only picture we have of Jesus is Scripture. There is no real account of the minutia of his daily life. This lack of detail almost leaves us with the impression that he did not have to deal with the same kinds of small choices that confront and sometimes confound us throughout our day. If we had a better picture of these details, we probably would feel more comfortable with the processes that went into his making the larger decisions: What should I say to the Pharisees? Should I turn the water into wine? Should I go into Jerusalem? We see these "choices" as flowing directly from the will of the Father, but we ignore the little details of the smaller choices that he had to make. If we simply see him as a kind of automaton operating on some form of externally-controlled auto pilot or as a puppet functioning at the end of strings attached directly to the Father's will, we end up with a picture of a man who is really not functioning as any man we know. We are, therefore, left with the compelling conclusion that he operated with *free will* just as we do, and he had to make choices just as we do. We then should assert that for a choice to be authentic, all the alternatives must be at least possible. From the point of view of free will, he would have to have been able to say *no* for his *yes* to be authentic—to have meaning.

Unfortunately it may not be as simple as this. If the way free will works itself out in the Godhead is a mystery, we need to be very careful how we talk about free will in the Son of God. In doing so, we need to be very careful about two different manifestations of the Son and the language we use to differentiate them: (1) the purely divine Son who is the second person of the Trinity, seated at the right hand of the Father—we will call him the eternal Son, and (2) the incarnate Son who took on a human nature during his mission on earth—we will call him the temporal Son. We are not talking about two different persons, but two different ways the Son is revealed or manifested and consequently two different sets of characteristics that are part of that revelation. Before we go too much further, we must understand that the relationships between these two manifestations are not exclusive, and understanding and articulating the way in which they are *not exclusive* has been and remains a central challenge for theologians trying to describe the Trinity and the Incarnation. For the purpose of this discussion, what we mean by the "eternal Son" is the incorporeal Son whose relationship to the Father and the Holy Spirit is captured in Trinitarian theology, and what we mean by the "temporal Son" is the enfleshed Son whose relationship to the Father and humanity is captured by the study of Christology. All of this tip-toeing around is designed to allow us to make one point in our discussion of whether Jesus could say *no* to the will of the Father. Our confusion regarding this question inevitably arises through a confusion of these two ways in which the Son has been revealed to us in Scripture. The question of Jesus' free will or his ability to make choices must refer only to the temporal Son who was operating out of his humanity in order to accomplish and reflect his own divinity—the same divinity that is exclusively operating in the eternal Son. Again, there are not two Sons but two ways in which the Son is revealed. Before and after the Incarnation, the eternal Son does not express himself through a temporal existence. In this case the will of the Father, Son, and Holy Spirit are by definition the same divine will. There is no possibility of there being any *choice* in a human sense in any of the three persons of the Triune God—no possibility of any disagreement. We might say that their wills are not only affectively one (in one accord) but ontologically one (of one essence). When the Son took on human flesh, a human nature, and a human will in the Incarnation, however, he placed himself in a different relationship to the Father—one of dependence. This dependence is reflected in the following statement:

> "I can do nothing on my own authority; as I hear,
> I judge; and my judgment is just, because I seek
> not my own will but the will of him who sent
> me." (John 5:30)

It would make no sense whatsoever to say that the eternal Son is in a dependent relationship to the Father in this way. This mystery is captured by the ancient understanding of the Trinity when we say, all of the Father is in the Son, and all of the Son is in the Father.

Understanding the relationship between the temporal Son and the Father is quite a bit more challenging. Theologians still struggle with the right way to understand this mystery and often have to invent new words to express the ineffable. What we can say here is that this dependent relationship of the temporal Son offers a possibility for God to show humanity how humanity was created to be in relationship with the Father. This relationship can only be shown by one who participates in this relationship himself. Thus Jesus must take on our human relationship to the Father—one of complete dependence—in order to show us what that should look like. It is only in this context that the *obedience* of the Son to the will of the Father takes on any meaning. It would make no sense to say that the eternal Son is obedient to the will of the Father. Unless we can at least conceptually separate these two ways of being in the Son, we cannot untangle the two ways of thinking about the question of the Son's free will, his ability to choose, and the possibility, as remote as it may seem, of his saying *no* to the Father.

Now, regarding the concept of *freedom*, we get a deeper picture of what is going on. We would have to assert that Jesus was not trapped from a "sin" point of view, so, in this sense, he was perfectly free. This freedom would have led him to choices that did not fall short of the will of the Father. He was perfectly surrendered to that will. Therefore, we could say that, while he had the God-given *free will* to make creative choices, his posture conditioned by his *freedom* from sin was such that the choices he made were always in accord with the will of the Father. In other words, he had the legitimate possibility of saying *no* but did not. He had the legitimate choice of being disobedient but chose rather to be obedient.

This idea that Jesus was obedient to the will of the Father is central to our understanding of who Jesus was and how he functioned. Consider the following:

> And being found in human form he humbled himself and became obedient unto death, even death on a cross. (Philippians 2:8)

One of the challenges we face when understanding Jesus is the tension between the idea of his being an automaton or a puppet and the idea that he was *obedient*. In the same way that a *yes* gets its authenticity from the legitimate possibility of a *no*, obedience gets it authenticity from the legitimate possibility of disobedience. For his obedience to *engage* us and draw us toward the same kind of obedience, it must have the same kind of context that our own obedience has, and there is simply no question that our obedience has as its context the often overwhelming attraction of disobedience. This is called temptation, and we know he was tempted as we are in every way, yet without yielding to that temptation—sin (see Hebrews 4:15). It is interesting and possibly compelling to see this *engagement* as precisely the basis for our understanding the concept of salvation. As much as we might want to see the salvation that is offered to us by the life, death, and resurrection of Jesus Christ as a kind of ticket to the heavenly arena, we are drawn to a deeper understanding by the very concept of obedience. All our efforts to answer the question of why God had to become man for us to be saved rest on the idea that God must *engage* us where we live in order to move us. It is something like a furniture mover trying to move a piece of furniture by *engaging* it in some lifting effort. Consider the following:

> And he withdrew from them about a stone's throw, and knelt down and prayed, "Father, if you are willing, remove this chalice from me; nevertheless not my will, but yours, be done." And there appeared to him an angel from heaven, strengthening him. And being in an agony he prayed more earnestly; and his sweat became like great drops of blood falling down upon the ground. (Luke 22:41-44)

The gut-wrenching obedience of Jesus engages us because it is exactly like those moments in our own lives when we are faced with a gut-wrenching choice in which the challenge of obedience versus disobedience is clear—the decision to give a child up for adoption, the decision not to use extraordinary measures to prolong the dying process of a loved one, the decision to let go of material things we hold dear in the face of financial difficulties, the decision to punish a child for something we fully understand as part of their own growing process—all of these can bring a certain amount of anguish. The challenge to do the right thing in trying circumstances is a problem of obedience, and the degree to which we can gain insight and strength from Jesus' own struggles is precisely the degree to which we are "saved" from making the wrong choice. Only if Jesus' struggles are real can they truly engage us.

Consequently, a perfectly orthodox answer to the question is *yes*, he could have said *"no"* because he had the same free will, or freedom of choice, as you and I have, and this gives meaning to his *yes* to the Cross—powerful, passionate, compelling, wondrous, life-saving meaning—and I would suggest that this meaning is worth fighting for. We simply cannot place Jesus on an inaccessible pedestal to the extent that he no longer can engage and thereby save you and me from a shabby excuse for a life.

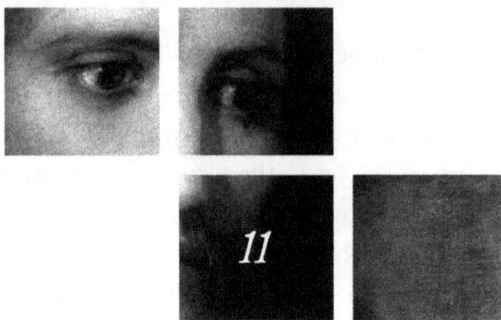

11

Miracles and Me

Under what circumstances, if any, can you walk on water?
Under what circumstances, if any, can you raise someone from
the dead?

We actually have been circling this very topic of miracles in many of the previous questions. The Incarnation of Jesus Christ makes him an intimate participant in our lives—as one of us. Thus, whatever we do, we cannot use the miracles to separate Jesus from us. If he is to save us, he has to be able to reach us, touch us, engage us, feel with us, fear with us, struggle with us, rejoice with us, weep with us, hunger with us, feel our pain and know our sorrows. We must at all costs protect that connection. But at the same time, Jesus is the Son of God, the second person of the Triune God—"God from God, light from light, very God from very God, begotten not made, consubstantial [of one substance] with the Father, by whom all things were made."[30] Thus, along

---

30 Nicene Creed, found in any Roman Catholic missal or Episcopal Book of Common Prayer.

with his humanity, we have to protect his divinity, which in some sense separates him from us infinitely. The miracles give us an opportunity to struggle with the interface between Jesus' temporal humanity and his eternal divinity. It is clear that his *humanity* was the first thing about him that his followers encountered, but how was his *divinity* manifest? What was his spiritual and mental posture in his relationship with the Father that could result in the occurrence of events apparently outside the laws of nature? If the majority of time the will of the Father for his Son was to "play the game," how do the miracles fit into this framework, and how should they fit into our own posture and framework? Finally, how are the miracles in both his life and our lives a reflection of something much larger—the way in which humanity can participate in the eternal life of God? All of these questions are embedded in the two questions asked above.

First let us look at a couple of very common answers to these two questions. One position is to shrink from the possibility of doing such radical things as the Son of God did. I might respond along the following lines: "I am not the Son of God; he was God and I am not." Therefore, the whole idea that I could possibly walk on water (that wasn't frozen) or more especially raise someone from the dead is absolutely ridiculous and demeans the power of the Son of God. We think that by taking this position, we are protecting the divinity of Jesus, and as we have said, we must do that. On the other hand, we could see the miracles as a natural extension of Jesus' relation to the Father that he offers to us. In this context we are challenged to figure out how we too are called to do the same kinds of miracles. In this case we protect his humanity and allow his humanity to elevate ours. We might say that the whole point that St. Maximus was making in Chapter 9 was that Jesus came to us precisely to draw us into the life of God. What evidence can we draw upon to clarify these two positions? Are they in fact incompatible, or can we understand the works of Jesus in such a way that their unique characteristics as the works of God are preserved while at the same time their characteristics as the works of a man keep them from separating him from us?

The most powerful statement by Jesus himself is the following:

> "Very truly, I tell you, the one who believes in me will also do the works that I do and, in fact, will do greater works than these, because I am going to the Father." (John 14:12)

Here we see a direct connection between believing in Jesus and doing works that not only equal but surpass the works that he did. Our first challenge is to understand what we mean by the word "believe." It would be convenient if belief in something were a black and white issue, regarding which everyone would agree when belief is either "on" or "off"—sort of like a light switch. I think we can all say from our own experience with the wide variety of folks who "go to church" that there is a host of motivations and therefore a host of levels of belief. This situation would look more like a rheostat that allows one gradually to change the level of light over the dining room table. Those who believe with every fiber of their being are clearly operating on a different level than those who believe enough to get to church on Christmas and Easter, but find their "spiritual" nourishment on the golf course or by curling up with the Sunday *New York Times*. Even the Devil believes that God exists—he just doesn't believe what he says is true. The Sicilian Mafia might be considered to be good Catholics, at least from a cultural point of view, but few of us would place their level of belief on a par with St. Francis or St. Teresa of Avila.[31]

So when is there enough belief for us to fall into the category to which Jesus is referring? Of course, this is not for us to know. This would require a level of "judgment" that appears to be reserved for God alone. What we do know from 2000 years of Christians struggling to receive all that Christ has offered us is that Jesus throughout his ministry referred to a radical transformation that would make us look very different from what we look like without him. What we can say here is that Jesus is not talking about lukewarm belief that leaves us unchanged but a "hot" belief that changes us radically. In fact, we might use the concept of *posture* to clarify the picture of a true believer: one who assumes a posture of willingness and surrender all the time. This is a tall order, and few of us would assert that we have arrived at that point, but at least we have an image of what Jesus was talking about when he used the word "believe."

The second twist in the quotation is the connection between his "going to the Father" and our call to do "greater works than these." One of the most profound aspects of the Incarnation is that it is limited in time. It has a start and an end. There is something essential about the end—this returning to the Father. We can capture some of this importance by making a distinction between a true faith and a cult. Many toss around the word "cult" as if it refers to any belief system that is radically different from their own. This

---

31   The scene in the movie *Godfather III* (Paramount Pictures, 1990) contrasting the baptism in the church with the murders going outside captures this incongruity perfectly.

relativistic definition seems to reduce its usefulness as an objective characterization. What might be a cult to you might be true faith to someone else.

Let me offer a more focused definition. In many instances a cult finds its central deviation from true faith inasmuch as it is tied to a living person—a leader who is both charismatic and authoritarian. The followers often give up control of their thoughts and actions to this leader. The members of the People's Temple in Jonestown, Guyana, were followers of Jim Jones. By the definition offered here, this would be called a cult. Members of the Branch Davidian religious sect in Waco, Texas, were followers of David Koresh. This would certainly fall under our definition of a cult. The "Manson Family," including Charles Manson and his followers, had the same characteristics. In this context, when someone alludes to a group of people as a cult, the first question is, who is their leader, and what role does he or she play in molding the followers' thoughts and actions?[32] We might note that the Pharisees who encountered Jesus and his followers would probably have called them a cult. The central characteristic of this understanding of the word "cult" is the fact that followers are bound to the teachings and authority of the charismatic leader to the exclusion of any rational or external test of truth or lie. The leader becomes the only test, and this circularity becomes the root of the dilemma for the followers.

---

32   In the Catholic faith, the word "cult" has a somewhat different meaning. The old meaning in a religious context refers to the veneration of or the religious practices that relate to a particular person. The root, "cultus" is from the Latin "to cultivate." The word "culture" has the same root. Thus, the cult of Mary refers to the veneration (holding her in high esteem—not worship) of Mary and the religious practices (devotion) such as the Marian Rosary that have grown up around her. As a word study, that of the word "cult" is rich and multifaceted.

Cults therefore are inherently dangerous, not necessarily by their specific beliefs, but because of the *posture* of the believers—a posture that is grasping and holding rather than surrendering and yielding, a posture that is easily manipulated and controlled rather than a posture that discerns truth from lie and is willing to stand for the former.[33]

What is happening in the quotation above is that Jesus knows at some point he must leave in order for his followers' trust in his concrete being to be transformed into true faith in the unseen God. He knows that our tendency as human beings to attach ourselves to a living leader gets in the way of our ability to transcend that local earthly relationship and be transformed into not only "followers" but also "reflections" of the leader. As long as the cult leader is around, the followers are bound to his or her words and actions as the central expression of their "belief." Jesus expresses this very understanding by saying that he must leave in order for his followers to grow into all that he has offered them.

The radical nature of this call is reinforced when Jesus admonishes his disciples:

---

33   Another interesting comparison is found in comparing the main legitimate religions of the world, whether Christianity, Judaism, Buddhism, Islam or Hinduism, and the New Age process of "channeling." On the surface the posture seems to be very similar to that of true prayer, and many can be drawn into these New Age practices for exactly that reason. In other words, posture is not enough. When I asked a friend what was it about Christianity that protected one in a posture of prayer from yielding to undesirable influences, his stern answer was "orthodoxy." In other words, the sacraments and doctrine of the Church inherently protect one who is in a posture of surrender. I must admit, his response lent a certain amount of additional weight to the concept of orthodoxy. This may be one reason why we are struggling so hard to find the orthodox answers to the questions on *The Quiz*.

". . .heal the sick, raise the dead, cleanse the lepers,
and cast out demons." (Matthew 10:8)

Here Jesus is simply carrying his words to their logical
conclusion, because these were precisely the "works" that he
did. By explicitly naming specific works, he left no doubt as
to the kind of transformation he intended for his followers.
We can be certain that his followers were astounded by Jesus'
assertion that they could in fact participate fully in the same
kind of relationship to the Father that he had, enabling them
to perform the same kinds of miraculous works that he did.
In other words, these passages show that Jesus clearly intended there to be continuity between his miraculous works and
the works of his disciples.

The next question that should be bursting forth is, did
they actually do these kinds of miraculous deeds? For this we
can look at the works of the Apostle Peter. Recall that the
only reason that Peter did not walk very far on water was his
lack of faith:

And Peter answered him, "Lord, if it is you, bid
me come to you on the water." He said, "Come."
So Peter got out of the boat and walked on the
water and came to Jesus; but when he saw the
wind, he was afraid, and beginning to sink he
cried out, "Lord, save me."

Jesus immediately reached out his hand and
caught him, saying to him, "O man of little faith,
why did you doubt?" (Matthew 14:28–31)

And Peter himself raised Tabitha from the dead:

Now there was at Joppa a disciple named Tabitha, which means Dorcas. She was full of good works and acts of charity. In those days she fell sick and died; and when they had washed her, they laid her in an upper room. Since Lydda was near Joppa, the disciples, hearing that Peter was there, sent two men to him entreating him, "Please come to us without delay." So Peter rose and went with them. And when he had come, they took him to the upper room. All the widows stood beside him weeping, and showing tunics and other garments which Dorcas made while she was with them. But Peter put them all outside and knelt down and prayed; then turning to the body he said, "Tabitha, rise." And she opened her eyes, and when she saw Peter she sat up. And he gave her his hand and lifted her up. Then calling the saints and widows he presented her alive. And it became known throughout all Joppa, and many believed in the Lord. (Acts 9:36–42)

The implication is that the followers of Jesus were expected to participate fully in the miracle-filled life of Christ.

So why do we have so much trouble seeing ourselves as the source of the same kinds of miracles Jesus did? Maybe it is because we have a very fuzzy understanding of the mode in which Jesus was functioning—the Incarnation. We need to understand that "source" and how it was accessed by Jesus in order to understand how we are to access that same source.

Recall in Chapter 7 that we made a connection between the will of the Father and the obedience of the Son. We could say that there are two ingredients for a miracle to take place: the will of the Father and the obedience of a faithful instrument of that will. In the case of the miracles Jesus performed, he was the faithful, obedient instrument. Here is a model for how one might think about this. Many mystics and theologians have talked about the fact that the divinity of Christ was "veiled."[34] It was there, and it was his, but it was not accessible to him in the same way it was when he was not bound by his earthly mission.

We can think of this veil as something like a Transitions Lens®, the opacity being controlled by the amount of light that interacts with the chemical composition of the glass. The more light there is, the more the lens darkens, thus letting in less light to the wearer. The "veil" might operate something like that. The opacity of the veil is dependent on two factors: the will of the Father and the obedience of the Son. In this case, however, the veil becomes *less* opaque to the Son as the two conditions are satisfied. In other words, in special cases when the Father wanted to glorify the Son and show who he was, the Father willed that the veil be opened. The obedience of the Son completed the circuit, so to speak, and Jesus had access for this specific work, to his own divinity and all the characteristics that accompany it. When the Father wanted the water turned into wine *by the Son* and the Son was the obedient instrument of the Father's will, the water not only became wine, but it became the best wine. For Jesus, the source of his divine powers was his own divine nature.

The same is true for walking on water and raising Lazarus from the dead. If the Father wanted to show the nature of the Son by his walking on water, and the Son was the

---

34   See, for example, "His divinity was hidden beneath the veil of His Humanity." Marmion, Blessed Columba, *Christ the Life of the Soul* (2005), Zaccheus Press, p. 179.

obedient instrument of the Father's will, *he was walking out there.* If the Father wanted Lazarus to be raised up from the dead through the Son, and the Son was the obedient instrument of the Father's will, *he was coming up.*

And therefore the same thing is true for you and me. Since with God all things are possible, if God wants you to walk on water for whatever reason, and you are an obedient faithful instrument of God's will, *you're walking out there.* And if God wants grandma raised from the dead through you, and you are the obedient and faithful instrument of that will, *she is coming up.* These are statements of faith. Our *posture* toward the will of God should be such that, if God wants it done through us—in other words, it is his will for us—and we are the faithful, obedient instruments of his will, then the supernatural powers of God can make something that operates outside the normal laws of the physical universe take place. It is a kind of tapping into the divine omnipotence of God in much the same way Jesus tapped into his own divine omnipotence to be an instrument of the will of the Father. Will that ever happen? I don't know. No one can know the time or place when God will want a miracle to occur through us. All we can do is to assume a posture of submission to his will, so that, if and when he does, we are not blinded by self-interest, fear, or timidity.

We often see the challenge of the Gospel story as one of factual belief or intellectual ascent, without understanding the point of the story. We think it is about obtaining a ticket to heaven when it is even more about the way we live our lives here and now. This "way" can often best be described as a posture of willingness—an openness to the possibilities that are before us to enrich our lives. This posture can be seen as one of prayer. Consider the following:

> Rejoice always, pray constantly, give thanks in
> all circumstances; for this is the will of God in
> Christ Jesus for you. (1 Thessalonians 5: 16-18)

We often stumble over the idea of praying constantly. Paul is clearly not talking about some external manifestation of prayer. He is not asking us to stay in church all day on our knees or to recite prayers as we drive along. He is telling us to assume a prayerful *posture* at all times, so that every choice we make and every resulting action is in accord with the will of God for us. This prayerful posture is precisely what sets up the possibility of our living fully into who we were created to be and tapping into the peace and joy of God.

While it may look like we can assume this posture of willingness on our own, one of the profound truths of the spiritual life is that the posture that allows us to access the gifts of God is itself a gift. When Jesus showed us his life in relationship to the Father as one of obedience and surrender, he was not only demonstrating what our lives should look like, but he was also making it possible for us to live it. In other words, he was offering us the gift of the possibility of a posture of willingness and surrender. We might think of this rather circular process as analogous to priming a pump. When one wanted to pump water from a well using an old hand pump, often one needed to prime the pump by pouring a cup of water in the pump to create the physical connection between the water in the well and the pump. When we assume a posture such as kneeling, we are simply priming the pump, because the true posture of prayer is a gift of God that is given to those who ask for it—in other words, to those who prime the pump. We can't take any credit for any aspect of prayer other than making ourselves available. As we explore the relationship of this posture to a life of constant prayer, we can see the same process at work. When we pray, we might prime the pump by assuming a prayerful posture such as kneeling or folding our hands and saying the words, "Dear God." Oddly enough the rest is a gift of God, even the process of asking for other gifts such as healing or strength or courage.

As we have explored previously, Jesus is the perfect model for our lives, and the miracles he performed were accomplished in precisely the same way we are called to perform miracles—as a function of the will of God and our own faithful obedience. Once we grasp this, the picture of what has been offered to us through Christ becomes clearer and clearer. But let us clarify a couple of little points.

When we speak of this direct correspondence between the will of the Father and the obedience of the Son, we must be careful not to see Jesus as merely a puppet of the Father, just as we must be careful not to see our ultimate goal as being little puppets of God. Jesus has a dynamic, creative relationship to the Father. Remember, sometimes the Father simply wants him to "play the game." By that we mean that there are choices we are called to make every moment of every day that determine a pathway from point A to point B. It could be a literal game that would entail how we get from the twenty yard line to the goal line at the other end of the football field, or it could involve how we drive from our own home to work every workday. The fundamental issue is the same. God gives us freedom to choose the details of our journey, even though we believe that there is a "big picture" that is compatible with who we were created to be—the will of God for us in this life. Tim Tebow, the former quarterback of the Denver Broncos, made an interesting explanation of his prayerful posture that he shows at various critical times during the game. He said he was praying that all his actions "honor God." He is not praying to win; he is praying that his life honor God. How can a completed forward pass honor God? How can an interception by the opponent honor God? When one prays for a life that honors God, he or she is praying for a life that is lived with love, truth and integrity—a life that has as its foundation a posture of surrender to the will of God. When God says to Jesus, "Play the game," he is saying, find the pathway that best exhibits a life that honors me through love, truth, and integrity. The details of how he does that are not necessarily preordained. This is certainly true for us as well. We too are called to play the game with love, truth and integrity, but also with creative possibilities concerning how we do that.

Thus, the miracles of Jesus show us how the various dimensions of the Incarnation—humanity, divinity, the will of God, and obedience—work together to result in works that manifest the activity of God in our daily lives. While we look forward to the promise of eternal life after death, we also are assured by the miracles of Jesus that the eternal life of God can be manifest here on earth right now, if God wills it and if we are the obedient and faithful instruments of that will. As we proceed along our journey toward oneness with God, we start to see the possibility of miracles all around us and to appreciate our own role in bringing them about. The miracles of Jesus are therefore a sign for all of us of the miraculous life of God that is offered to us through Christ.

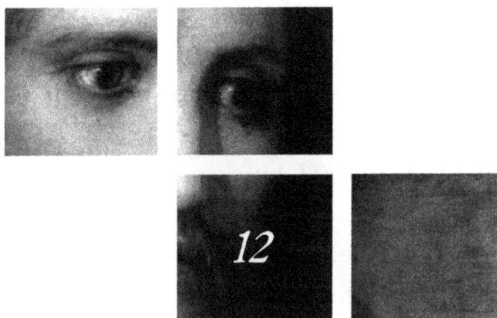

Humanity

If we say that Jesus was "one substance" with the Father,
what was his relationship to us?
If Jesus was "fully human and fully divine," does this mean that
his humanity was somewhat different from ours?

A s much as the Apostles tried to be clearly understood
when they wrestled with the Incarnation, and as much
as the Church has tried to live up to its responsibility as
guardians of the Apostolic faith, the fact of the matter is we
still don't have it figured out. If you are Catholic, Episcopalian (Anglican), Methodist, or Lutheran, you would be familiar with the Nicene Creed, which states that Jesus Christ
is "one being with the Father"[35] but says little about his relationship to us except that he was "made man."[36] We have

---

35 The new Catholic translation of the Latin Mass uses the uses "consubstantial with the Father", a closer rendering of the Latin words *"consubstan-*
tiálem Patri."

36 See the *Book of Common Prayer* of the Episcopal Church, p. 326 or *The*
Catechism of the Catholic Church, p. 49 - 50.

Scripture that points toward a profound relationship to us, but sorting it all out was and continues to be a challenge. Operating from Scripture alone requires one to replicate all the struggles of the early Church in sorting out complexities and even the inconsistencies of Holy Writ. Where should we start? The two questions point us in three critical directions. The first is the relationship of the Son to the Father. This we would find in what is known as Trinitarian theology—the study of the way the Father, Son and Holy Spirit express the deepest meaning of the Godhead. The second is the relationship between the Son and us. This we would find in the special Christian anthropology that would be described in the study of Christ or Christology. The third is the relationship between Jesus' humanity and his divinity. This too would be discussed under the topic of Christology, but would focus on how these two fundamentally different characteristics of Jesus could coexist in one human being—or one divine *person*.

We should start by trying to understand the phrase "one substance," and this is no simple task. The early Church struggled with the right words to use to describe the incarnate Lord's relationship both to the Father and to us. The discussion centered on the distinction between general characteristics that could be shared and particular characteristics that made one unique. Here are some words that entered into the debate: *prosopon* (Greek for person), *persona* (Latin for mask, character, personality), *hypostatsis* (Greek for substance), *ousia* (Greek for essence), *substancia* (Latin for essence), *charakter* (Greek for nature) and *physis* (Latin for nature). Each of these words has subtle implications in their respective languages, and the early writers often used the same words to mean different things and different words to mean the same things. It is interesting in this regard to note the three words: hypostasis, substance and understand. All three mean to "stand under." The specific meaning must be taken from the way each is used in its respective language. In this debate, we must go even further and take the meaning from the context and way in which the words were used in the debates of the early Church. The first refers to the individuality of the three persons of the Trinity. Thus, there are three hypostases or persons, the Father, Son and Holy Spirit, in the Triune God. The second refers to the essence or nature of the Godhead, of which there is only one. In other words, each person of the Trinity shares the same substance. These two relationships form the foundation of Trinitarian theology. The third word, of course, is an English verb for the process of capturing the meaning of something and played no role in the debate. It is not our purpose here to work through the entire debate but to create some context for our understanding of the complexity of the idea of "one substance." The problem being addressed was the question of how Jesus was like the Father and how he was different from the Father. In Trinitarian theology, the Son is the second person of the Trinity. He is like the Father in his essence or substance (thus "of one substance") and is unlike the Father in that he is a different person with different characteristics. In this case the central different characteristic is that the Son is "eternally begotten of the Father before all the worlds."[37]

Now that we have a handle on the premise of the first question, we can start to address the question itself. Here we are first suggesting that there is a relationship and that understanding it is central to being a Christian. The way in which Jesus relates to us is the very foundation of how he is able to influence our lives. We call this influence *salvation*. We have

---

37 Ibid.

repeatedly alluded to the fact that Jesus' intimate relationship
to us is precisely the factor that allows his life to engage ours
and thereby become both a model and a means for our new
life that better reflects who we were created to be. We are
now trying to fill out more specifically what that relationship is.

What are some possible responses to this first question?
On the one hand, one might respond in such a way that up-
holds a perceived fundamental difference between Jesus and
the rest of us. One might reply that Jesus was God and we
are not. Of course the phrase "one substance" asks for a response in terms of the same concept. We might, therefore,
say that he was *not* one substance with us because his divinity made him essentially different from us. While some
might think this would be a poor and unfounded position to
take, let me assure you, it is very common. While comparing yourself to Jesus might be taken to be the most basic expression of our Christian walk, such audacity is often viewed
with disdain. For example, if someone suggests that you are
being too disruptive, you might assert that Jesus himself as
part of his mission on earth was *disruptive*—the mere fact of
being disruptive does not necessarily mean that what is going
on is not of God. The quick-draw response designed to keep
you in your place might be to state that, "Yes, but Jesus was
God and *you* are *not*." If one is to hold to this understanding,
one must emphasize the *differences* between Jesus and you and
play down the *similarities*. To support this approach we might
look for evidence in Scripture.

There are plenty of opportunities to see drastic differences.
Jesus was born of a virgin and you and I were not. Jesus did
many miracles that most of us see as vastly different from how
we live our lives. Jesus was raised from the dead physically,

and we understand our own resurrection on a more spiritual plane. And finally he ascended to heaven, right before the Apostles' very eyes. While the Apostles first encountered his humanity and had no problem understanding that the one whose ministry they observed and participated in was a man, the story as it is presented to us in Scripture offers many opportunities to separate him from ourselves. In particular the Gospel of John takes our understanding of Jesus' relationship to the Father to a whole new level.

> In the beginning was the Word, and the Word was with God, and the Word was God. He was in the beginning with God; all things were made through him, and without him was not anything made that was made. In him was life, and the life was the light of men. The light shines in the darkness, and the darkness has not overcome it. (John 1:15)

Paul also develops an understanding of Jesus that clearly supports his intimate relation to the Father.

> . . .yet for us there is one God, the Father, from whom are all things and for whom we exist, and one Lord, Jesus Christ, through whom are all things and through whom we exist. (1 Corinthians 8:6)

> Then comes the end, when he delivers the kingdom to God the Father after destroying every rule and every authority and power. (1 Corinthians 15:24)

And finally Peter states:

> For when he received honor and glory from God
> the Father and the voice was borne to him by the
> Majestic Glory, "This is my beloved Son, with
> whom I am well pleased." (2 Peter 1:17)

One has little problem appreciating the difficulty that
some might have in seeing Jesus as one of us—an ordinary
human being. In fact, once we understand and state repeatedly that he was one substance with the Father, he becomes
less and less ordinary and more and more different from us.
We are therefore torn between these many clear references to
his divinity and the somewhat more subtle references to his
humanity. If we were to err, most of us would tend to err on
the side of his divinity.

On the other hand, you might see a level of intimacy that
Jesus intends between himself and his followers. You, therefore, might stretch to find words that express that intimacy.
You might even take a leap and assume that he is "one substance" with us without really knowing what that means. It
would be nice, however, to be able to authenticate your response. In looking for any opportunity to connect the incarnate Lord with our human lives, you might search Scripture and the documents of the Church to find something that
would shed light on what the Church had formulated over
the last 2000 years.

As we have mentioned before, there are also plenty of passages in Scripture that point clearly toward Jesus' humanity.
He wept, he was hungry, he slept, he was wounded, and he
died. As we have seen, writers such as Paul and the author
of the Letter to the Hebrews try to make very clear that his

humanity was just like ours. We might even go so far as to say that he had "ordinary" humanity. In other words, what the followers of Jesus encountered was in many ways an "ordinary" human being. Now of course we know that we all as unique individuals run the gamut from highly talented to less than remarkable, but in some deeper sense we are all ordinary human beings. My humanity is the same kind of humanity as everyone else's. What we find in Paul's letters and in Hebrews is a development in the Gospel story that tries to clarify this very point about Jesus. Unfortunately, this was not enough for the early Church. There was still considerable confusion.

One of the great efforts to nail down who Jesus was in his earthly ministry was the Council of Chalcedon in A.D. 451. Finally we had a clear statement, though actually it still took hundreds of years for folks to agree on what this profound statement meant. Because of its importance and its relative brevity, I quote it in its entirety:

> Therefore, following the holy fathers, we all with one accord teach men to acknowledge one and the same Son, our Lord Jesus Christ, at once complete in Godhead and complete in manhood, truly God and truly man, consisting also of a reasonable soul and body; **of one substance (homoousios) with the Father as regards his Godhead, and at the same time of one substance with us as regards his manhood; like us in all respects, apart from sin;** as regards his Godhead, begotten of the Father before the ages, but yet as regards his manhood begotten, for us men and for our salvation, of Mary the Virgin, the God-bearer (*Theotokos*);

one and the same Christ, Son, Lord, Only-begotten, recognized in two natures, without confusion, without change, without division, without
separation; the distinction of natures being in no
way annulled by the union, but rather the characteristics of each nature being preserved and coming together to form one person and subsistence,
not as parted or separated into two persons, but
one and the same Son and Only-begotten God
the Word, Lord Jesus Christ; even as the prophets
from earliest times spoke of him, and our Lord
Jesus Christ himself taught us, and the creed of
the Fathers has handed down to us.[38]

The key words (bold) for our purposes are "of one substance (*homoousios*) with the Father as regards his Godhead,
and at the same time of one substance with us as regards his
manhood; like us in all respects, apart from sin." While we
often stress Jesus' relationship to the Father, we often for-
get to give equal weight to his relationship to us. This relationship to us, in fact, is the point of the Incarnation. Recall
what St. Maximus the Confessor said:

The sure hope of the deification of humanity is
the Incarnation, which makes of man god in the
same measure that God became man.[39]

In other words, God draws near to us in order to draw us
near to himself. This simultaneous intimate relationship of

38　*Book of Common Prayer*, 1979, Seabury Press, p. 864.
39　Palmer, G. E. H. et.al., ed., *The Philokalia*,1986, Faber and Faber, Inc.,
Winchester, MA, v. II, par. 62, p. 177.

Christ to both the Father and us is precisely the key to the Incarnation.

Why should we care about this simultaneous relationship of Jesus to the Father and to us? As we have said before, the fullness of our own lives somehow depends on our access to the fullness of life itself. If we understand God as simply the source of all love, truth and life, and if we see our personal difficulties as those aspects of our lives that disconnect from that source, then it becomes clear that inasmuch as Jesus is a bridge to the life of God, he offers us that access. He thereby saves us from a life that falls short of what has been offered to us—he offers us *salvation*. It really doesn't require any profound surrender to something that some would call magic. It simply is common sense. You and I don't want to settle for the shabby stuff of life when we can have the good stuff. Here is a real man that offers us that life. How precisely all the wires are hooked up and all the circuits work is indeed a mystery, but the fundamentals are really not so obscure. Common sense really comes in handy here.

We now have the tools to answer the second question. The Council of Chalcedon goes to great, even sometimes convoluted, lengths to answer this question unequivocally. The key statement here is "recognized in two natures, without confusion, without change, without division, without separation; the distinction of natures being in no way annulled by the union."[40] In simple terms this means that it is appropriate to say Jesus was human—period. That is a true statement and can stand on its own. It is just as appropriate to say Jesus was divine—period. That is a true statement and can stand on its own. Thus, when we say Jesus was "fully human and fully divine," we do not mean "fully-human-and-fully-divine"

40 *Book of Common Prayer*, 1979, Seabury Press, p. 864.

in some kind of combo state of being that requires a form of agglomeration of the two states of being. Simply put, the answer is *no*, his humanity is not different from ours in any way. Of course another attempt to make this absolutely clear is the statement, "like us in all respects, apart from sin." It is still a wonder why we continue to try to pry Jesus away from ourselves by attributing to him characteristics that are clearly not human. If one considers all the scriptural references, the writings of the early Church Fathers and the conclusions of the early councils, there has been a remarkable effort to make sure that we see Jesus' humanity as just like ours, and yet we continually find some kind of perverse solace in swimming upstream against these efforts. It may be that we find it somewhat comforting to find a way to discount his message by creating an insurmountable gap between Jesus and ourselves. Ironically, it is precisely the same kind of gap between man and God that Jesus clearly came to bridge.

Again, the reason why this is of fundamental importance to us is that it is the mode of our salvation or our return to a life in communion with God or the best life we were created to live. This union of humanity and divinity, as Maximus points out, is precisely the union that brings about the possibility of the union of our own humanity with the divinity of God.

In addition to this union of our own personal humanity with the eternal life of God, there is an even more profound union that takes place upon the ascension of Jesus to the Father. Since Jesus takes our humanity with him upon his ascension to the Father, the human nature of Christ is now, therefore, a part of the Godhead. This has been called by some the *Trinification* of humanity. It is based on pieces of Scripture like the following:

But he [Stephen], full of the Holy Spirit, gazed
into heaven and saw the glory of God, and Jesus
standing at the right hand of God; and he said,
"Behold, I see the heavens opened, and the Son
of man standing at the right hand of God." (Acts
7:55-56)

He thus makes a home for our very nature in the Godhead. Our kinship with God is made even stronger as a result
of the Incarnation. We might say that through the Incarnation and Jesus' ultimate return to the Father, Jesus has paved
the way on a number of fronts for our return to a life that
participates fully in the eternal life of God, not only after we
die, but also *right now*—the amazing life of love, truth, peace,
and joy we were created to live.

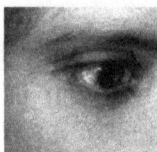

Sin

How good can you be?
Can you be without sin?
If you cannot be without sin, which sins are considered
acceptable to the Father?
In light of the death and resurrection of Jesus,
are you still a slave to original sin?

These questions explore the same kinds of issues we've been looking at: *Who was Jesus and what has he offered us?* When we ask, "How good can you be?" we are inquiring about the yardstick you use for your life. What is your model? One answer I have heard is, "as good as I can be." I am not sure how this response informs anything, since it is perfectly circular, but it does point out a major difficulty with the question. The first question has to do with the nature of goodness. We think of goodness as an active characteristic that centers on doing good things: baking cakes for others, holding the door, smiling, sharing, saying kind things about someone else, petting the dog, and so forth. So to ask how good one can be is to ask how many good deeds one can cram into one's day. It sounds like a daunting task that might prompt a circular and innocuous response to the question. If, on the other hand, goodness is a state of being out of which flows good deeds—some would call these *fruits*—then we are forced to ask for some model for this state of being. What is the model that we would use as the ultimate picture of goodness? Is it Abe Lincoln or George Washington or Moses or Mary or St. Francis or Socrates? Could it be my Mom or Dad, my Grandmother Fletcher or my next door neighbor? Do the tools of our various faiths help us address this question? Let me offer a little story in this regard. I recall musing over this question one afternoon when my UPS driver, Asia Ferguson, arrived to deliver a package. Knowing he was a music minister at a small Baptist church in Springfield, South Carolina, I thought I would try out this question on him. I can see his response as if it were yesterday. He got this gentle smile on his rich, textured, kind black face, rocked back on his heels, looked a little skyward and with great relish said, "As good as Jeeesus." Well, there you have it. No sacraments, no writings of the great ecumenical councils, no confession of faith, no magisterium, no Pope, no bishops or priests to keep him in theological line, no Church Fathers or Luther or Calvin or Wesley to set out the doctrinal basics from which to draw. With only Scripture and an abiding faith in Jesus Christ, *he got it*—in all its fullness—no hesitation, no confusion, no silly circular answer—just the Spirit-filled truth of God, blossoming forth from this simple man of God. Now, let me be clear. I am not saying that the Church and sacraments and a deposit of faith are unimportant. It is only by and through some authority that we know Asia was right. I am just saying that the truth is accessible to all who seek it. It is amazing that the more complex the liturgical and doctrinal basis of our faith, the more confused we get about questions as simple as this one. We should assert, however, that we, with all the tools of salvation at our disposal, should know better and live out more clearly than anyone the fact that we are called to nothing less than the full goodness of Jesus Christ.

Now that we know the model for goodness, we need to ask whether that model is indeed accessible to us. Was Asia right? Can we be as good as Jesus? One approach to this question is to address the second question above. One of the problems is the issue of sin itself: what is it? Most Christians take it for granted that we understand the nature of sin, but when we get down to the nitty gritty, we often disagree on what exactly constitutes sin. Technically the definition of sin from an ancient Greek perspective is captured in the word *hamartia*, which means, "missing the mark." In this case, if Jesus is the model, then he becomes the mark—the bull's eye on the target. To the degree that we miss this bull's eye, we miss the mark—we fall short of who Jesus was in his most general characteristics of truth, love, and integrity and thereby fall short of who we were created to be. So, to ask whether we can be as good as Jesus is really the same question as whether we can hit the mark. Can we *not* sin? As one looks at the history of the Church from its earliest years, through the Reformation, and to the present, this question has been pivotal in characterizing the doctrinal differences in the various Catholic and Protestant churches.

Let's poke at this issue a little. Many of us feel that we are somehow constrained, for one reason or another, from being completely good. We are told that we are sinners, which is true, and that we will always be sinners, which might be true. The technical term for the propensity to sin is *concupiscence*. It is a consequence of original sin—one that many, particularly many Protestants, believe cannot be washed off. This creates an impenetrable barrier to complete goodness. In other words, not only do we sin, we *must* sin. We simply can't help it. As an antidote to this dismal condition, some traditions have developed a doctrine of "imputed righteousness," which means that even though we are stained by our sinfulness, God imputes a level of cleanliness or righteousness to us. God sees us as if we were sinless even though we are not. Unfortunately we are somehow left with the dilemma of answering the question with something other than a purely trivial response. As we will see from some of the other questions, this approach gets boxed in pretty quickly.

On the other hand, others understand the whole Gospel story as one about the gift of righteousness to a mankind who had lost it in the Fall of Adam and Eve from which we get original sin. A general term for these churches would be "holiness churches"—churches that hold that we are not only called to be holy—without sin—but that holiness has been made available to us through the life and death of Jesus Christ. The Pentecostal Holiness Church, the Wesleyan Church, and the Catholic Church all fall into this category.[41] In these cases the understanding is that our goodness is only limited by our ability to avoid sin, assuming that is even possible. To do this, we must believe that sin is not inevitable. To expose this challenge, it is helpful to understand some of the process by which we as individuals fall into sin.

There are three general ways that this process begins: (1) we take our eye off the mark, just like a distracted archer, (2) we flinch or allow some extraneous event to move us off

---

41 Let's not kid ourselves here—many pastors and members of these churches fail to understand the radical beliefs of their own traditions.

the mark, just like an archer buffeted by the wind, or (3) we are not strong enough to stay on the mark, just like an archer who is out of shape. Inattention, external influence, and weakness are triggers that can start us down the path of sin, and we are not talking just about big sins like murder, rape, addiction, or making "porn." It may be as simple as thinking ourselves the source of our own talents (pride), eating too much at dinner (gluttony), or not getting enough exercise (sloth). But none of these occur all at once. We have mentioned the triggers, but then what? The process is well known—it is called the slippery slope. The more we allow ourselves to get drawn into a kind of unhealthy behavior, the easier it is to get drawn in again and again and the harder it is to stop. I recall hiking up Table Rock near Greenville, South Carolina, one summer afternoon. When I reached the top, I found that I was looking over a huge granite slope that very gradually got steeper and steeper until it plunged off the side of the mountain. (This would be a South Carolina "mountain.") It was just fascinating to start to walk out over the slope and find the apprehension growing. The point at which I stopped was the point at which I became uncertain whether there were forces of gravity that might just overcome my purchase so that I could no longer reverse my path. This was so funny because it was so far from what one might consider "the edge." There was no question that I could have moved out further toward the edge without any danger, but my sense was that I didn't feel comfortable doing so. It was all so gradual that I felt as if I could be deceived. So I played it safe and kept my distance. There is no better metaphor I can think of for the slippery slope. The only difference was that I could see the slope gradually fall off before me, and I was able to make a rational decision when to stop. Unfortunately unhealthy behavior does not show us a clearly defined slope, and consequently we rarely know when to stop. That is why sin is so dangerous: it is not that an individual action will take us over the edge; it is that we don't know which action is the one that does. Where is the point of no return? Where is the point at which we go tumbling over the edge of Table Rock?

Let's return to this idea of concupiscence. Even though we may believe concupiscence is a reality, it is not necessarily an impenetrable barrier. While some might believe it is, we might counter with the belief that through the help of God, all things are possible. Consider the following:

> But Jesus looked at them and said to them, "With men this is impossible, but with God all things are possible." (Matthew 19:26)

From this piece of Scripture, we definitely get some hope that we are not stuck in a rut. But the immediate question is, how do we access the power of God to penetrate this barrier of concupiscence? As Christians we would say through faith in Jesus Christ, the barrier can be pierced. Piercing the barrier of our inclination to sin is simply another angle on the idea of salvation. We are saved from being trapped by sin through the life and death of Jesus Christ.

> . . .and from Jesus Christ the faithful witness, the first-born of the dead, and the ruler of kings on earth. To him who loves us and has freed us from our sins by his blood. . . (Revelation 1:5)

> . . .but if we walk in the light, as he is in the
> light, we have fellowship with one another, and
> the blood of Jesus his Son cleanses us from all sin.
> (1 John 1:7)

His life gives us a model, and his death gives us access to
that model. When we finally realize that we have only one
model—Jesus Christ—and that he has given us all he was as
the incarnate Son of God, the one who was just like us, yet
without sin, then we are on the road to shedding the sins that
keep us from the eternal life of God.

We have likewise addressed the second question. If we
can be as good as Jesus and Jesus was without sin, can we
be without sin? There are at least two interpretations of the
term, "without sin," we need to explore. One interpretation
refers to a state of being without sin all your life. We could
safely say that all Christians would agree that at least one person did not sin all his life—Jesus.[42] But there is another interpretation of the phrase "without sin." We could think of
it as meaning to be without bread or your keys or a raincoat.
In this case we mean that we are without something at this
moment. In this sense we are simply asking, can you *not* sin?
Both Jesus and Paul, throughout their ministries, admonish
folks not to sin. The implication is that it is possible *not to
sin*. In fact, the early interpretation of the Church was that it
was a place for saints—those who did not sin. Only gradually did it become clear that this was easier said than done,
and the Church gradually became seen as a school for sinners.
All this does not change the admonishment of Jesus and Paul.
While we would be hard pressed to find anyone who in one
way or another did not sin, our faith tells us that sin is not a

---

42   Catholics would assert that Mary too was without sin her whole life.

necessity, and the capacity not to sin has been offered to us through faith in Jesus Christ.[43]

Thus we come to the next question; namely, the improbability of the idea that some sins are OK with God. Let us see what we can find in Scripture to point us in the right direction. Here is an exhaustive, and some may say exhausting, enumeration of all the possible sins:

> Now the works of the flesh are plain: fornication, impurity, licentiousness, idolatry, sorcery, enmity, strife, jealousy, anger, selfishness, dissension, party spirit, envy, drunkenness, carousing, and the like. I warn you, as I warned you before, that those who do such things shall not inherit the kingdom of God. (Galatians 5:19-21)

> And since they did not see fit to acknowledge God, God gave them up to a base mind and to improper conduct. They were filled with all manner of wickedness, evil, covetousness, malice. Full of envy, murder, strife, deceit, malignity, they are gossips, slanderers, haters of God, insolent, haughty, boastful, inventors of evil, disobedient to parents, foolish, faithless, heartless, ruthless. Though they know God's decree that those who do such things deserve to die, they not only do them but approve those who practice them. (Romans 1:28-32)

> Do you not know that the unrighteous will not

---

43   And the Catholics would add: through the sacraments of Holy Baptism, the Eucharist and Reconciliation, which are a product of that faith.

inherit the kingdom of God? Do not be deceived; neither the immoral, nor idolaters, nor adulterers, nor sexual perverts, nor thieves, nor the greedy, nor drunkards, nor revilers, nor robbers will inherit the kingdom of God. (1 Corinthians 6:9-10)

But fornication and all impurity or covetousness must not even be named among you, as is fitting among saints. Let there be no filthiness, nor silly talk, nor levity, which are not fitting; but instead let there be thanksgiving. Be sure of this, that no fornicator or impure man, or one who is covetous (that is, an idolater), has any inheritance in the kingdom of Christ and of God. (Ephesians 5:3-5)

Put to death therefore what is earthly in you: fornication, impurity, passion, evil desire, and covetousness, which is idolatry. On account of these the wrath of God is coming. In these you once walked, when you lived in them. But now put them all away: anger, wrath, malice, slander, and foul talk from your mouth. Do not lie to one another, seeing that you have put off the old nature with its practices and have put on the new nature, which is being renewed in knowledge after the image of its creator. (Colossians 3:5-10)

. . .understanding this, that the law is not laid down for the just but for the lawless and disobedient, for the ungodly and sinners, for the unholy and profane, for murderers of fathers and

murderers of mothers, for manslayers, immoral persons, sodomites, kidnapers, liars, perjur-
ers, and whatever else is contrary to sound doctrine, in accordance with the glorious gospel of
the blessed God with which I have been entrust-
ed. (1 Timothy 1:9-11)

For men will be lovers of self, lovers of money,
proud, arrogant, abusive, disobedient to their
parents, ungrateful, unholy, inhuman, implaca-
ble, slanderers, profligates, fierce, haters of good,
treacherous, reckless, swollen with conceit, lovers of pleasure rather than lovers of God, holding
the form of religion but denying the power of it.
Avoid such people. (2 Timothy 3:2-5)

Whew! Well, if you can't find yourself in there somewhere, you probably are not breathing. What does this tell
us about God's attitude toward sin? While it must be inferred
from all the references in the Bible, it is pretty clear that that
all sin is repugnant to God, and it is hard to see God as satisfied with some minor level of sin.

. . .that you may be blameless and innocent, children of God without blemish in the midst of a
crooked and perverse generation, among whom
you shine as lights in the world. . . (Philippians
2:15)

God, therefore, wants us to be sinless, spotless, without
blemish, even though in the past we may have wallowed
in sin. That is why forgiveness is a central characteristic of

Christians and mercy a central characteristic of God. For Catholics the sacrament of Reconciliation is of central importance. For Episcopalians the sacrament of confession exists. The edict "all may, some should, none must" is operative here. For other Protestant churches personal relationships with both God and others are always seen in the context of forgiveness. Consider the following story of Jesus and the woman caught in adultery:

> The scribes and the Pharisees brought a woman who had been caught in adultery, and placing her in the midst they said to him, "Teacher, this woman has been caught in the act of adultery. Now in the law Moses commanded us to stone such. What do you say about her?" This they said to test him, that they might have some charge to bring against him. Jesus bent down and wrote with his finger on the ground. And as they continued to ask him, he stood up and said to them, "Let him who is without sin among you be the first to throw a stone at her." And once more he bent down and wrote with his finger on the ground. But when they heard it, they went away, one by one, beginning with the eldest, and Jesus was left alone with the woman standing before him. Jesus looked up and said to her, "Woman, where are they? Has no one condemned you?" She said, "No one, Lord." And Jesus said, "Neither do I condemn you; go, and do not sin again." (John 8:2-11)

This story has three important protagonists: the accusers,

the woman, and Jesus. As we put ourselves in the place of each of these, we see the incredible importance of forgiveness in our lives. Ultimately all of the various understandings of the importance of forgiveness, particularly the forgiveness of God, are designed to point us to the fact that forgiveness has the power to wash us clean so that we may go forward and "sin no more."

Finally we come to a question that directly addresses the inevitability of sin. For most Christians this all hinges on one's understanding of original sin and its accompanying concupiscence. There are two obvious positions: (1) that we are stuck and (2) that we are not stuck. Here is a powerful piece of Scripture that points to the first:

> If we say we have no sin, we deceive ourselves,
> and the truth is not in us. If we confess our sins,
> he is faithful and just, and will forgive our sins
> and cleanse us from all unrighteousness. If we say
> we have not sinned, we make him a liar, and his
> word is not in us. (1 John 1:8-10)

Here is the problem with which we are faced: Is John's statement *descriptive* or *prescriptive*? Is he telling us how it is or how it has to be? Many would say that he is being prescriptive and stating very clearly that we simply cannot *not* sin. Others would say that he is being descriptive, since probably none of us have met anyone who has not in one form or another fallen short of the perfection of God. All we can do here is look at a couple of traditions and make a choice. As we said earlier, the general Protestant tradition would choose the first and the Holiness tradition would choose the second. Since I am clearly coming from the latter tradition and am trying to lay out how these pieces fit together in *The Quiz*, let me explain the second a little further. For Catholics, the sacrament of Holy Baptism has one major effect—it cleanses us not only of all prior sin but also of the stain of *original sin*. Of course we know that, if we are at an age where we can take responsibility for our own actions, we can jump right back into a pattern of sin, but the stain of *original sin* has been removed forever. Original sin, as formulated by the Church Fathers, is a state of fallenness, resulting from the actions of Adam and Eve, that makes it impossible for us *not* to sin. We are thus slaves to sin from the moment of birth. There is simply nothing we can do about it. Try as we might, we still get stuck, and it is inevitable that we do so. Baptism, on the other hand, removes the stain of original sin. In other words, after Baptism we no longer *have to sin*. It has been said that before Baptism we cannot *not* sin, after Baptism we *can* not sin, and in heaven we *cannot* sin. In other words, any Christian who has been baptized[44] and "washed in the blood of the lamb" is no longer enslaved to sin. We have been enabled or *grown up* to take responsibility for our own *falling short*.

However you understand the concept of original sin and even if you think the concept is not particularly compelling, at some point in your journey toward fullness of life, you must take responsibility for your falling short of what God created you to be. We can no longer blame anyone else—least of all God. That is the maturity of an adult Christian. By analogy we could recall that when we were children, we were admonished to look both ways before crossing the road. If our parents did not teach us or weren't looking out for us,

---

44   It is worth noting that the Catholic definition of a Christian is "anyone who has been baptized *with water* in the name of the *Father, the Son and the Holy Spirit.*"

it was their responsibility. But when we became adults, we had to take responsibility for our own actions, only blaming ourselves if we failed to look both ways. In other words, Jesus grows us up and turns us into mature human beings who not only must take responsibility for our actions, but also who have been given all the tools to do so. For Catholics that tool is the sacrament of Holy Baptism. For others it may be simply the realization that I am saved by the power of the life, death and resurrection of Jesus Christ. More particularly, the way this happens is through the action of God in our lives. Jesus speaks directly about sending a source of understanding and action in our lives:

> "Nevertheless I tell you the truth: it is to your advantage that I go away, for if I do not go away, the Counselor will not come to you; but if I go, I will send him to you. And when he comes, he will convince the world concerning sin and righteousness and judgment: concerning sin, because they do not believe in me; concerning righteousness, because I go to the Father, and you will see me no more." (John 16: 7-10)

> "When the Spirit of truth comes, he will guide you into all the truth; for he will not speak on his own authority, but whatever he hears he will speak, and he will declare to you the things that are to come. He will glorify me, for he will take what is mine and declare it to you. All that the Father has is mine; therefore I said that he will take what is mine and declare it to you." (John 16:13-15)

It turns out that the source of that action in our lives here and now is the Holy Spirit. It is the Holy Spirit that infuses our lives with truth, wisdom, and love that allows us to forego sin and live the life we were intended to live from the very beginning. This is one way of stating the Good News of Jesus Christ: the *eternal life of God*, a life in perfect accord with the will of God—no deviation, no sin, a life of complete fullness—*has been made perfectly available to us* through Jesus Christ and the Holy Spirit he sends to us to fill us with the spirit of the truth and love of God.

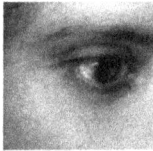

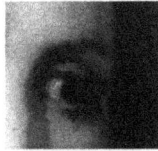

14

Faith

Did Jesus have faith? How much?
How much faith can you have?

As we have said before, and this is a good time to practice our little tool, we can ask the question, "What do
we mean by *faith*?" Since our whole discussion will center on
the answer to this question, let us first explore some different possibilities of what we may be referring to when we use
the term "faith." Let us first look at a few of the ways Jesus
used the word faith: "your faith has made you well" (Matthew 9:22), "oh you of little faith" (Matthew 14:31), "if you
had faith the size of a mustard seed" (Matthew 17:20), "if you
have faith and do not doubt" (Matthew 21:21). We could also
note Jesus used the word "believe" in much the same way—
the opposite of doubt—when he was talking with Thomas.
After Thomas convinced himself of the truth of the resurrection by placing his fingers in Jesus' wounds, Jesus said to
him, "Have you believed because you have seen me? Blessed
are those who have not seen and yet have come to believe"

(John 20:29). We first see that the words *faith* and *belief* are often used interchangeably. If we are careful, we will be able to do this in what follows. We also see that there appear to be at least two connotations associated with the word *faith*: intellectual and spiritual. Let us consider each.

In the first case, we have faith *that* or believe *that* something is true. This involves an intellectual assent. We believe something we cannot corroborate with sensory evidence. I may have faith that I was not adopted. I might believe that Santa Claus exists. I could believe that my car will be ready from the mechanic by this evening at 5:00. I might have faith *that* the watch is really a Rolex and not a cheap imitation. I could have faith *that* the sun will come up tomorrow or *that* my next step will be on firm ground just like my last. Faith of this kind is embedded in every thought we think and every action we take. In fact, this faith is reflected in the limitless assumptions we make about our lives. Mother will continue to love me. Dad will continue to protect me. Our home will still be there tomorrow. We will continue to have enough to eat. These last assumptions are particularly important for children who must depend on others for their very survival. In fact, the assumptions we make or the things that we believe to be true become more and more important as we become more and more dependent. These kinds of situations involve those recovering from serious injury and those who are old and infirm. This dependency becomes particularly important as we consider our spiritual lives.

In the spiritual realm, I could have faith *that* Jesus was God or *that* what he said was true. This kind of faith is still one of intellectual assent. It has to do with knowledge. We might say that we have faith *that* God exists. Again, this kind of faith believes something to be true—a factual statement.

Thomas had a problem with this kind of faith when he doubted the resurrection of Jesus. Jesus was alluding to this kind of faith when he spoke of those who doubted that he was the Son of God. As we get a clearer picture of this kind of intellectual assent, we might just find that many of us are limited to this kind of faith. Our minds operate as if these things are true, but our faith never makes it out of our minds. We take aspects of the Christ story as assumptions on which we base our lives—at least at some level—but we are not changed at a deeper level.

But there is a different sense of having faith: faith *in* something rather than faith *that* something is true. In this sense, faith is more like *trust*. I might have faith in my auto mechanic. I could have faith in the fidelity of my spouse. I might have faith in the ability of my periodontist to do a good job. I could have faith in my investment banker (not that I actually have one) that he is not running a Ponzi scheme. This is a much less specific kind of faith. In other words, I trust my spouse to be true to his or her vows, my periodontist to be a competent surgeon, and my investment banker to be honest. This kind of faith is not so much an intellectual assent but a surrender, a yielding. We use the phrase, "I put my trust in you," as a way of expressing that surrender. I give up control to you and give you influence over my life. If I were an astronaut, I may believe *that* the rocket will work, but when I jump aboard and place my life in the hands of the engineers and mission controllers, it is a whole new ballgame. This now requires a very different posture of trust than the trust I have in my auto mechanic. My very life is at stake. I must put my trust or faith *in* them.

As we move into the spiritual realm, I might say that I have faith *in* God in the sense that I put my whole trust in

God. This is not so much an intellectual *assent* (an agreement) to the existence of God as it is an *ascent* (a climb) of the heart. This kind of faith involves my whole life and wellbeing. My faith *in* Jesus Christ is not so much an intellectual assent but a spiritual ascent. It raises me to a new level of reality and experience that is only possible by assuming a totally new posture of surrender and trust. As a result of this new kind of faith, we do what may appear to many as strange things: we spend time in church and not on the golf course or the tennis courts; we get down on our knees and say things to someone who isn't there in any corporeal sense; we sing songs about Jesus, put our arms around each other, and maybe even put our hands on their heads when they are in distress of one kind or another. Strange indeed! But if one is unable to move from the assent of the mind to an ascent of the heart, one is certainly unable to understand what in the world is going on.

While these two understandings of the word *faith* are intimately related, they operate from different centers: one is intellectual and the other is spiritual. One is of the mind and one is of the heart. One reason that we might not separate the two is that someone cannot engage in one form without some aspect of the other. Our intellects are intimately related to our spiritual posture, and our spiritual posture influences the degree to which we make ourselves available to certain intellectual possibilities. It is impossible to trust God if we don't believe that God exists. In other words, it is impossible to have faith *in* God unless we have faith *that* God exists. These two ideas of faith—one of the mind and one of the heart—are essential for an overarching faith characterized by a posture of willingness and trust, specifically a willingness to be transformed into who God wants us to be. This is precisely the same kind of trust the astronauts have when they put their complete trust in others, becoming totally dependent on the people who designed and built the rocket and those who will control the mission. In fact, to be willing to be changed into someone different takes even more trust. Consider this kind of trust:

> Now there was a man of the Pharisees, named Nicodemus, a ruler of the Jews. This man came to Jesus by night and said to him, "Rabbi, we know that you are a teacher come from God; for no one can do these signs that you do, unless God is with him." Jesus answered him, "Truly, truly, I say to you, unless one is born anew, he cannot see the kingdom of God." (John 3:1-7)

> But if we have died with Christ, we believe that we shall also live with him. (Romans 6:8)

> He himself bore our sins in his body on the tree, that we might die to sin and live to righteousness. By his wounds you have been healed. (1 Peter 2:24)

This idea of dying and being born again is the most radical trust one can have. To put one's life totally in the "hands" of God is to have total faith of the second kind—an ascent of the heart that leaps and soars to new heights of love and truth that only comes from a life in and through Christ.

To have this kind of faith, we need to start with the faith *that* the eternal life of God has been made available to us through Christ. Likewise we need to have faith *in* God's plan for us in order to surrender to such a plan. The combination of faith of the mind and faith of the heart yields a posture of surrender to the will of God in order to be changed into the person we are intended to be.

With this clarification, we can start to address whether Jesus had faith and, if so, what kind. In order to answer this, we need to take a step back and look at the issue of faith as it relates to the *beatific vision* discussed in Chapter 6. If one assumes that he continually experienced an immediate vision of God, then one would be hard pressed to assume that he needed the faith of the first kind. The only problem with this is a troublesome statement that he makes regarding the end times:

> "But about that day and hour no one knows, neither the angels of heaven, nor the Son, but only the Father." (Matthew 24:36)

As we discussed above, this would appear to imply that there were factual things (in this case the timing of the second coming) of which Jesus did not have knowledge. Now some would say that he said this because he was not intended to reveal the day and hour. However, this understanding does not really address the question as to whether he knew the day and hour but was not intended to tell his followers, or whether he genuinely did not know the day or the hour because the Father had not revealed it to him. If we continue with our "veil" model, we could assume that he was not intended to reveal it and therefore the will of the Father had not given him access to that information. If this is true, we could say that, because there were things that Jesus did not know, he was operating at least to some extent on the faith of the first kind. There was some degree of intellectual assent to things unseen. We should also assert, however, that he would not have had faith of the intellect regarding essential aspects of his being and his mission. Those were known clearly. It is this aspect of faith that many are referring to when they suggest Jesus did not have or need faith.

Now we get to the Garden of Gethsemane and the following quotation:

> Then he said to them, "I am deeply grieved, even to death; remain here, and stay awake with me." And going a little farther, he threw himself on the ground and prayed, "My Father, if it is possible, let this cup pass from me; yet not what I want but what you want." (Matthew 26:38–39)

Let's not be too glib about the transition from "let it pass" to "what you want." This quotation probably should contain some pauses between these two statements, if we are to take his struggle seriously. There most likely was some time in which Jesus awaited the Father's response. If Jesus already knew what the response was, then he was really wasting everyone's time with the empty request. In truth, his struggle was real. We can assume this because he repeats the prayerful request:

> Again he went away for the second time and prayed, "My Father, if this cannot pass unless I drink it, your will be done." (Matthew 26:42)

And here is another set of verses found only in the Gospel of Luke:

> Then an angel from heaven appeared to him and
> gave him strength. In his anguish he prayed more
> earnestly, and his sweat became like great drops
> of blood falling down on the ground. (Luke
> 22:43–44)

Unless this is a staged display of anguish, we must accept
the fact that the writers of the Gospels believed Jesus' struggle the night before his crucifixion was real. If we too accept
this reality, then we must see his obedience as a profound
trust in the will of the Father. The fact that he saw the excruciating end awaiting him—and still went forward with it—
is plentiful evidence that he trusted the Cross not only was
necessary, but also was the will of the Father. We then could
unequivocally assert that Jesus exhibited a faith of the heart
characterized by a posture of complete trust in the Father.

One additional quotation from Scripture is interesting in
this regard:

> . . .looking to Jesus the pioneer and perfecter of
> our faith, who for the joy that was set before him
> endured the cross, despising the shame, and is
> seated at the right hand of the throne of God.
> (Hebrews 12:2)

The word "pioneer" points toward one who set a pathway in the very same context in which we are called to travel.
The pioneers were not simply those who got there first but
those who blazed the trail. They showed the way with the
very same limitations that others would have who followed
them. A space man who showed up in California in the early 1800's would not have been called a "pioneer." He might

have gotten there first, but the way he got there would have been totally foreign to the way others would travel and the hardships they would have to endure. Calling Jesus a pioneer of our faith is a clear indication that the author of Hebrews saw an intimate connection between the faith of Jesus and our own faith. He was not only the pioneer of our faith but also the perfect model for it. If we want to see what perfect faith looks like, the author of Hebrews tells us to look at Jesus.

Be advised that there is a whole school of thought that would summarily dismiss the idea that Jesus had any faith of either kind. Before we address this, we should note that these same theologians would say that Jesus did not experience the virtue of *hope*. Here we can go to Paul for a commentary on hope:

> For in hope we are saved. Now hope that is seen
> is not hope. For who hopes for what is seen? But
> if we hope for what we do not see, we wait for it
> with patience. (Romans 8:24–25)

Again we can see that the beatific vision would pretty much preclude Jesus having this kind of blindness. To see God "face to face," as we will see him in heaven, implies that there would be no veil to block communication or understanding. One might suggest that there would be nothing *unseen*. But we are still confronted with the idea that there were things the Father did not reveal to the Son. Although the distinction is not always clear, one might say that faith is predicated on a lack of direct knowledge in the present, and hope is predicated on a lack of direct knowledge of the future. We have *faith that* or *faith in*, and we *hope for*. If the model of the

veil that is controlled by the will of the Father and the obedience of the Son exhibits some fundamental qualities of the
relationship of the incarnate Son and the Father, then we can
see how Jesus could at times express extraordinary knowledge of the past, present and future as willed by the Father,
while being limited in his knowledge of other areas that the
Father did not wish to reveal to him as a part of Jesus' normal humanity. In other words, the will of the Father much
of the time is "play the game" and live your life as other human beings have to. Struggle as they have to, feel sorrow as
they have to, and suffer as they have to. In other words, place
your entire life in my "hands." Trust that my will for you as
a human being is the path of eternal life—even as the horror
of that path becomes clear. In other words, as Jesus got closer
to the crucifixion, the game got tougher and tougher. Jesus'
willingness to endure the suffering of the cross is directly related to his trust in the will of the Father.

So why would some be reluctant to ascribe the faith of the
heart to Jesus? It is difficult to see the Son of God in any need
of trust, especially if we tend to understand the Incarnation
more as an action of the divine nature than the human nature. Many who see the union of the divine and the human
natures in Jesus as allowing characteristics of the divine to
"leak" over into his human activity, tend to ascribe to him
extensions of human qualities such as knowledge and power
that take him outside the boundaries of normal human existence. To the extent that we do this, we are likely to discount
the possibility of his exhibiting any characteristics that smack
of human limitation, including the need for faith of any kind.

If the reluctance to ascribe either faith or hope to Jesus is
in any way legitimate, then we are confronted with a profound paradox. How can Jesus be a model for our lives in

every way and not have experienced two of the most important of the three theological virtues—faith, hope and charity—the virtues that take us to God? One way around this
is the way we have taken in the past. When confronted with
the dilemma of how Jesus can be the second person of the
Trinity for whom faith and hope have little meaning and at
the same time be a model for our lives in which faith and
hope are central to his life as a human being, we might be
forced to answer, "I don't know." But in saying this we assert with total confidence that both are true. Somehow he
is the model of faith and hope, exhibiting the posture of a
faithful and submissive servant who has the capacity to pray
to the Father with the same posture of faith and hope that
he desires for us. How this works itself out theologically, we
might have to leave to the theologians. But we cannot afford
to leave to the theologians the possibility of stripping us of
the perfect and complete model for humanity informed by
the supernatural divinity of our Lord and Savior Jesus Christ.
I would just ask the theologians not to abandon the mystery
of paradox in order to try to solve problems that may not be
solvable in this life.

We might get some insight into this dilemma, however,
by looking for a link between the virtue of charity or love
and the virtues of faith and hope. There would be no disagreement that Jesus is the model for our love of each other. The question we are asking here is whether we can find
some fundamental link between the love of God and how
Jesus models this for us in the posture of faith and hope. We
might start by asking what this posture is and how it might
apply to all three virtues. To love as God loves requires us
to be in communion with God to the extent that we sense
the "when and where and how" of God's love in particular

situations. The love of God could at times drive the money changers from the temple. The love of God might admonish the Pharisees about their hypocrisy. The love of God might be the tough love of intervention in the case of a drug addiction. The love of God might be at one moment tender and the next firm. The only way to know how to love as God loves is to be in communion with the source of that love—God. But what is required to be in that kind of communion? It is called prayer, and it requires a posture of surrender to the will of God—the very same posture of surrender we see in the posture of faith and hope. So here we can make a bold statement: it is impossible to exhibit the love of God without the posture of faith and hope. They are so intimately intertwined that they cannot be separated. Consequently, it is impossible to say that Jesus loved as the Father loved and did not experience the posture of surrender of faith and hope necessary for him to access the will of the Father that ultimately determined how the love of the Father would be expressed. I guess you would have to call this some form of theology, and it may be highly inadequate to the task, but it does point us toward a methodology that always requires that any answer we give regarding Jesus must take into account the fact that he must in some way be a model for our lives. At no time can we imagine going up to him and asking him a question about our struggles with faith or hope and receiving the bland answer, "Well, I have no idea what you are talking about. I don't have to worry about that." This is a ridiculous response, if I may be so bold, and is totally unworthy of the very foundations of the Incarnation. It may not be easy, but we simply must do better than this.

To get back to the questions, therefore, we can assert that a legitimate orthodox answer to the first question is that Jesus exhibited faith of the heart and in doing so showed us the proper posture for faith of the mind. Therefore, we would affirm that Jesus had faith and that his faith was complete. In addition, if it is true that Jesus offers all of himself to us and is the perfect model for our lives, then he offers us the possibility of the same complete faith he had.

As is always true, this is important because our understanding of Jesus offers us an understanding of ourselves as God created us to be. To live fully into the will of God requires that we live fully into the life of Christ—including a complete faith, which reflects the eternal life of God.

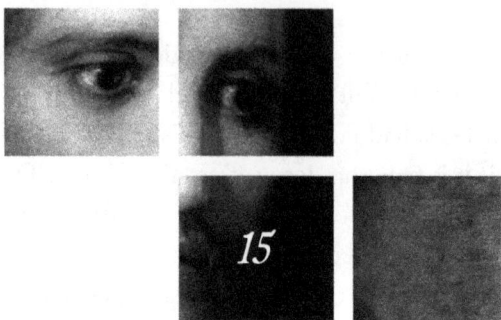

Glory

How much glory has been offered to you?
How much divinity has been offered to you?

One of the primary problems we encounter in answering these questions is exactly what we mean by the term "glory"—especially when we think of the person of Jesus. The fact that he was often painted with a halo not only points us to some kind of wonder that surrounded him, it also helps to confuse the matter. Then there are words we tend to use in order to capture some of this sense, such as magnificence, grandeur, and resplendence. How are we to make sense of the term "glory" in order to tackle the questions at hand?

In the case of Jesus, let us try to sharpen the discussion. Jesus has the glory of God. This is the sort of thing that is hard to put one's finger on, but clearly has the sense of being as much glory as one can manifest. The glory of God is what makes us stop in wonder and awe and become transfixed. If we take the glory of an unusually spectacular harvest moon (if you have never seen one, you may be at a disadvantage here)—a *huge* ball of fire rising in the east as the sun sets in the west—and multiply that many times, we may start to reach the limits of our human capacity to apprehend that which is infinitely greater and more beautiful than we are. We might say that the concept of glory is particularly human in its context; it has to do with the way we see things. I recall standing at the foot of one of the World Trade Center towers and looking up right along the side of the building. The view was so overwhelming and awe inspiring that it could literally take one's breath away—it was breathtaking. It may be impossible to think of God's glory as some kind of objective attribute that can be measured with a pyrometer[45] or Geiger counter. We do seem to sense that it functions at the limits of our ability to comprehend with our minds and apprehend with our hearts the otherness, transcendence, and breathtaking *je ne sais quoi*[46] that is God. We might say as a working definition that glory is that which inspires awe—takes our breath away.

Jesus clearly applies this concept to himself, as in the following passages:

> Glorify your Son so that the Son may glorify you. (John 17:1)

> So now, Father, glorify me in your presence with the glory that I had in your presence before the world existed. (John 17:5)

---

45   A pyrometer is a device that measures temperature as a function of the color—for example, white hot is hotter than red hot.

46   This is French for "I don't know what."

Now, the verb "to glorify" is even more challenging, because Jesus is implying that the glory of the Father is a gift only given by the Father. We assert that indeed the Father has given the Son his own glory to the degree that he, in his humanity, has the capacity to receive and show forth the glory of God. Theoretically we probably should say that the glory granted the Incarnate Son is, in fact, the same glory granted to the Eternal Son from before the beginning of time and made available to him during his earthly ministry—through the "veil" that is mediated by the will of the Father and the obedience of the Son. So the glory "granted" to the Son is, in fact, his own glory as the second person of the Triune God. Therefore, the question addresses the issue of how much of God's glory has been granted through the Son to his followers.

Why do we even ask such a question? We might assume that glory is something particular to God and has nothing to do with us in our mundane human lives. It is hard for me to think of myself as a carrier of God's glory, let alone that I might glorify God by anything I might do. So my first impulse would be to answer, "none," or perhaps I might hedge my bets and say something like, "a little." I hope you are starting to see such fuzzy answers for what they are—fuzzy. Jesus would have had none of this silliness.

What about the alternative? Could he possibly have given us more than we could imagine? Here is the critical piece of Scripture:

> The glory that you have given me I have given them, so that they may be one as we are one. (John 17:22)

It doesn't get any clearer than that. The answer to the question is that all of the glory granted the Incarnate Son has been, through him, granted to us. That is all well and good, but what does it mean to have the glory of Christ? I think we can start to access the power of this gift as we move through the other questions, because glory is simply one way of thinking about the nature of God and in particular his Son on earth. To the extent we shine forth the face of Christ, we show the world the glory of Christ and thus the glory of God. But what does all this really look like? We actually have some pointers that clarify how exactly the glory of God is manifest in Jesus. First we see that the glory of God is shown forth through Jesus' humanity. Jesus in the Incarnation gives humanity a whole new makeover. Humanity is no longer separated from God but now is taken into the Godhead, becoming the carrier of the bursting forth of God's glory on earth.

> And the Word became flesh and dwelt among us, full of grace and truth; we have beheld his glory, glory as of the only Son from the Father. (John bore witness to him, and cried, "This was he of whom I said, 'He who comes after me ranks before me, for he was before me.'") And from his fullness have we all received, grace upon grace. For the law was given through Moses; grace and truth came through Jesus Christ. No one has ever seen God; the only Son, who is in the bosom of the Father, he has made him known. (John 1:14–18)

More specifically, glory is manifested by love. In the Old

Testament, one of the many ways in which the glory of God is recognized is by steadfast love.

> Not to us, O LORD, not to us, but to thy name give glory, for the sake of thy steadfast love and thy faithfulness! (Psalm 115:1)

> The LORD appeared to him from afar. I have loved you with an everlasting love; therefore I have continued my faithfulness to you. (Jeremiah 31:3)

But how is this glory manifest in Jesus? While he clearly shows us the glory of God in different ways, the primary one, unifying all the others, is his love. It is so central to his entire mission, his whole mode of saving us from a life that massively falls short of the possibilities offered to us, that he offers us his own love, which just happens to be the love of God. It is so important that he puts forth a new commandment.

> "A new commandment I give to you, that you love one another; even as I have loved you, that you also love one another. By this all men will know that you are my disciples, if you have love for one another." (John 13:34–35)

And to complete the circle:

> He who does not love does not know God; for God is love. (1 John 4:8)

Notice that we will not be recognized by our piety, our

humility, or our joy, although all these are important parts of who we are called to be, but we will be recognized by our love. We now have a linkage from the glory of God as expressed by God's love for humanity, to the glory of God in Christ as expressed by his love for us, to the glory of God in us that we shine forth by our love for God and for one another.

The second question concerns how much *divinity* has been offered to us. If we recall that Jesus' divinity is an essential part of his very being—his personhood—but that it is veiled and is made manifest as the will of the Father and the obedience of the Son cooperate during the earthly mission of the Incarnate Son, then we have a model for relating our lives to that of Jesus.

Divinity is the eternal life of God—the quality of God that makes God who he is. It is his "Godliness"—his holiness. Here are some pieces of Scripture that point us in the direction of an answer:

> "Sanctify them in the truth; your word is truth. As you have sent me into the world, so I have sent them into the world. And for their sakes I sanctify myself, so that they also may be sanctified in truth." (John 17:17–19)

> "I in them and you in me, that they may become completely one, so that the world may know that you have sent me and have loved them even as you have loved me." (John 17:23)

First, we need to know the central importance of John chapter 17, the priestly prayer of Jesus made at the Last Supper

right before he was arrested, tried and crucified. Along with
his instruction to the Apostles, this prayer, only found in this
Gospel, gives the most direct statement of his intentions for
us. There is no way to prove the extent of his meaning. The
pointers are all there, but it has taken the Church many years
to formulate a clearer understanding of these pieces of the divine mystery. Here are some critical quotations from Scripture and the Church Fathers, those who were instrumental
in the early Church in articulating the meaning of Scripture,
taken from the *Catechism of the Catholic Church*:[47]

> The Word became flesh to make us partakers of
> the divine nature. (2 Peter 1:4)

> For this is why the Word became man, and the
> Son of God became the Son of man; so that man,
> by entering into communion with the Word and
> thus receiving divine sonship, might become a
> son of God. (Irenaeus)

> The only-begotten Son of God, wanting to make
> us sharers in his divinity, assumed our nature, so
> that he, made man, might make us gods. (Thom-
> as Aquinas)

So what does it all mean? At least some level of divinity
or the eternal life of God is what was given to humanity at
our creation. According to Genesis, we were created in the
image and likeness of God. The Church Fathers took this
to mean that the image of God was reflected in the characteristics of God that were given to us so that we could be in

---

47   Lebreria Editrice Vaticana, 1997, paragraph 460.

relationship with God—free will, an intellect, a capacity for love and truth, and so on. The likeness of God was taken to be the use of those characteristics to be *like God* in the sense of loving like God to the degree that humans can do that, thinking like God to the degree that humans can do that, acting like God to the degree that humans can do that, and so forth. In other words, we not only have been given the ability to be in communion with God but also the capacity to be who we were created to be, fulfilling our full potential in intimate relationship to our creator.

This relationship was broken by pride, whether you think of it as an historical event in the Garden of Eden or as an expression of a reality that continues to permeate our lives. Pride, or the illusion that we can operate as autonomous entities without each other and without a deep connection to a larger truth that we call God, is at the core of our problems as human beings. Thus, we started out in communion with the divinity of God; we had been given that communion as a part of the image and likeness. When we decided to go it on our own, we lost the likeness and with it our connection to the divinity of God.

The mission of Jesus Christ in the Incarnation is to restore this lost likeness and thereby this lost connection to God's divinity. Thus Jesus, the human being in full communion with the divinity of God and in full communion with the humanity of mankind, brings together humanity and divinity as it was intended to be from the beginning. What is not so obvious is that Jesus takes us even further than the original state of Adam and Eve. Not only are we restored to the original image and likeness, but we are even taken further into the eternal life of God. Before Jesus, humanity was not an integral part of the Triune God. After the Incarnation, humanity is actually taken into that eternal life. Jesus does not abandon his humanity upon his return to the Father but retains it as he sits at the right hand of the Father as the second person of the Trinity. We are now allowed an even more intimate relationship with God than was offered to Adam and Eve.[48] The difference this makes is one of degree. If we find our value as human beings in the fact that we were created in the image and likeness of God, and Jesus restores that which was lost in the Fall—the likeness—then that value is enhanced by the full effect of the Incarnation. It is said:

> My little children, I am writing this to you so that you may not sin; but if any one does sin, we have an advocate with the Father, Jesus Christ the righteous; and he is the expiation for our sins, and not for ours only but also for the sins of the whole world. (1 John 2:1-2)

This ongoing relationship between Jesus and us that persists even after the ascension is, therefore, a source of clarity and encouragement. Our own goal is made clearer by the path that Jesus takes back to the Father, and the means of making our way toward that goal is strengthened by Jesus' advocacy. The ultimate goal is to live a life in perfect communion with God—a life that reflects not only the life of Jesus' humanity, but also the same divinity that he manifested on earth. We would call this a supernatural life.

---

48   See Chapter 12 on the trinification of humanity.

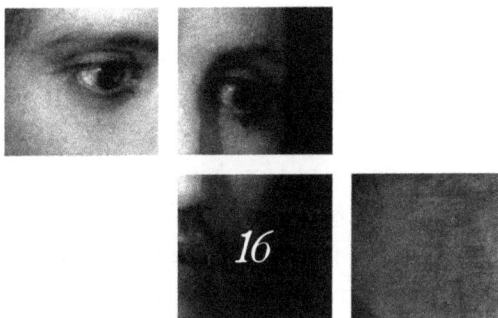

16

One

*Is it possible for you to be one with the Father as Jesus was
one with the Father?
How much like Jesus are you called to be?
How is Jesus different from you?*

All of these questions address the way in which Jesus relates to us. Consider the following:

> ". . .that they may all be one; even as thou, Father,
> art in me, and I in thee, that they also may be in
> us, so that the world may believe that thou hast
> sent me. The glory which thou hast given me I
> have given to them, that they may be one even as
> we are one, I in them and thou in me, that they
> may become perfectly one, so that the world may
> know that thou hast sent me and hast loved them
> even as thou hast loved me." (John 17:21-23)

The mission of Jesus in the Incarnation was to make us

one with the Father, but what is "oneness?" When Jesus says, "I and the Father are one" (John 10:30), many folks then and now take that to mean that Jesus and the Father are "one and the same." As a matter of fact, Martin Scorsese in his movie adaptation of Nikos Kazantzakis' *The Last Temptation of Christ* has Jesus saying precisely those words. This is a stretch of the Hebrew meaning of oneness. The Day of Atonement (at-one-ment) is a day intended to bring the people of Israel back into a state of oneness with God. Oneness was taken to be a state of accord—alignment—in right relationship—righteousness. So, whether or not we believe as Christians that Jesus was in reality God, what he *says* is that "I and the Father are in perfect accord." While that is still a bold statement, it does not necessarily mean, "I am God." We get that profound relationship from the whole ethos of the Incarnation events. One statement does not a profound mystery make.

But we do know from John 17 that Jesus intends for us to be in a state of oneness with the Father in precisely the same way that he was in a state of oneness with the Father, and since his relationship to the Father is one based on divinity, it is not a stretch to take that to mean that we are called to participate fully in his divinity. What do we mean by this? We find some help from the Church Fathers in the statement, "What he was by nature, we are called to be by grace."[49] This idea was known as the divinization or deification of humanity and meant that our lives were made divine by participation in his life. The possibility that this participation is intimate enough to be called divinity itself is part of the mystery

---

49   Although this is a very famous statement, it is not clear who first made it. It has certainly made its way into the theology of the early church as described by later writers such as Augustine and Aquinas.

of the Incarnation. In fact, a Latin term, the *admirabile com-mercium* or wondrous exchange, refers to the way in which the divinity of Christ is transmitted to his followers. One cannot precisely or quantitatively pin down what this means other than to say that it makes the divine life of Christ and thus the divine life of God available to us. It is through this process that oneness with God is made possible through Jesus Christ.

In this context we can address the next question. If we are to be one with the Father in the same way that Jesus was one with the Father, then we are called to be *just like Jesus.*[50] This involves a process of profound transformation from a state of sin to one of perfection through the gifts given to us through Jesus Christ and through the transforming action of the Holy Spirit. In other words, it is appropriate to say that we are called to be **transformed into the perfect likeness of Jesus Christ**, so that when someone sees us they see the face of Christ. This is not just a transformation of actions, as we said before, but a transformation of *being.* We are not called simply to take on the actions of Christ but, as Paul says, we are called to take on the *mind* of Christ (Philippians 2:5). The words "perfect" and "likeness" are carefully chosen, because many believe that we are called only to *grow* in our likeness or our holiness. Growth is certainly an essential part of the process of transformation, but the goal is *not* growth; the goal is the *perfect likeness.*

Let me make this abundantly clear. The goal of every Major League baseball team is *not* to grow in "winningness," but to win the World Series. The goal of every NFL team is *not* to grow in "winningness," but to win the Super Bowl. Why

---

50   You might be interested in a book by Max Lucado, *Just Like Jesus,* 2000, Word Publishing, Nashville, 223 pp.

we insist on a fuzzy goal is not clear. Maybe we think we can grow toward the goal, but we do not believe we can actually *reach* the goal. But here is one thing for certain: You cannot reach a goal that you have not set. The first goal of any Major League baseball team or NFL football team is to *believe* they can go all the way. *Believe!* Likewise, you absolutely will not reach perfection in Christ if you do not *believe* it has been made available to you—and not just available, but *perfectly* available. To take on this radical understanding is to take on a radically new posture, one that opens up greater possibilities—the possibilities Jesus intended for us.

This might be a good time to clarify the difference between what has been offered to us and what we can appropriate or access during our own lifetimes. While I am suggesting that the goal is clear and unequivocal, the process of attaining that goal is anything but straightforward. Those who thought that the goal could be gained by their own actions and efforts were called Pelagians, whose teaching was rejected by the Church as early as the fifth century when it was first articulated. Although this book is not intended to be a handbook for the process of transformation, I would be remiss if I did not make a few statements about the nature of the process itself. This process of transformation involves availing oneself of the mysteries Jesus ordained, such as Holy Baptism and the Lord's Supper. This path of transformation also involves an ongoing struggle against the temptations that draw us away from a rich spiritual life in the context of a vibrant community of faith. I am not saying it is easy. I am just saying that without a clear picture of the goal and the implied accessibility of that goal, the journey is an aimless wandering.

So while our goal is the perfect likeness of Jesus Christ

that has been completely offered to us right here and now, the process by which we make our way toward that is unlimited. This is clearly a paradox. Is it available or not? If it is available, then why can't we get it? Well, this is a little tricky. If Jesus was in a growing, dynamic, creative relationship to the Father, and we call that perfection, then our own perfection can only be found in our own growing, dynamic, creative relationship to God. We will never be able to say, "Whew, I made it," even though we say unequivocally that the perfection of Christ has been made perfectly available to us right here and now. This posture of total submission to the life we were intended to live looks just like the posture of Christ to the life *he* was intended to live on earth. Thus, we are really searching for the posture of Jesus—the mind of Christ (Philippians 2:5). It is not without profound importance that many of the parables Jesus tells concerning the kingdom of heaven have to do with growth: the parable of the seeds sown in different environments (Matthew 13:3–23), the parable of the weeds and wheat (Matthew 13:24–30), and the parable of the mustard seed (Matthew 13:31–32). Somehow growth is intrinsic to the goal without being the goal. Jesus is the goal, which is the same as saying that God is the goal. If we take our eyes off that goal, we could easily spend our time in activities like "going to church" that do not change us. It is interesting that some understand one sin against hope is *presumption*, and one form of that sin is the belief that we can receive forgiveness without conversion. Another way to say this is that it is presumptuous for us to think that we will attain to the gifts that God has offered us without being changed into the people he intends for us to be— into the likeness of Jesus Christ. We may not complete the process of transformation in this life, but we are called to be hip-deep in it to the end. We could say that it *could* be completed in this life because it has been offered to us, but it *will* be completed in the next.[51] That is our faith, and that is our hope on which we base all of our thoughts and deeds.

Here is another paradox to ponder. The goal is often seen to be somewhere "out there" some distance from where we are, but we should understand that the goal in some profound sense has already overtaken us. At our Baptism, we have been infused by the Holy Spirit who makes all of Christ intimately available to us as if it were already part of us. We can think of it like receiving a new lung, and the Doctor says, "So BREATHE!" Jesus might be saying to us, "Breathe in what is already yours." Or it might be like a child prodigy who has an incredible soprano voice that she has never had the confidence to use. Everyone knows she has it. All they can do is to encourage her to "Sing, my dear, SING!" Jesus might be saying the same kind of thing to us, "Sing out, my dear, with the voice of love and truth that already has been given to you!" This intimacy of goal and process makes the whole thing quite a mystery, and yet a more joyful and hopeful mystery could not be conceived.

Now, what about the difference between Jesus Christ and me? Well, this is really an open-ended question and can have many answers, but some are clearly wrong. If you dwell on the idea that he was God and you are human, you have missed the whole point of the Incarnation, but there *are* some differences. As the late Cynthia Deberry-Freeman, a marvelous and powerful preacher in South Carolina, used to say, "Jesus was first born, and we are n^{th} born."[52] But we are called

---

51   That is, of course, if you don't end up in the hot place—but that's another story for another time.
52   She was the founder of Abundant Life Outreach Ministries in Cayce,

to look the same as he did. Jesus is the vine and we are the
branches, but recognize that the vine and branches all look
the same when examined by themselves. If someone showed
you a skinny piece of a vine and a thick piece of a branch,
you would not know how to tell which is which. Jesus was
called to be the savior of the world, and we are called to participate in the process of salvation by being his hands and ears
and eyes on earth. Jesus was a divine person in the Chalcedonian sense, and we are human persons, but when he was in
his earthly ministry, he functioned as we do. Remember too
that he was "like us in all respects, apart from sin," so you
can't carry the differences too far, or you will throw out the
incarnational baby with the bath water. Clearly his divinity
is infinitely different from our humanity, but through his Incarnation and the *admirabile commercium* (wondrous exchange)
he offers us full participation in that divinity. Recall that the
Church Fathers would say that what he was *by nature* we are
called to be *by grace* (a free gift of God). Now, when we look
at how he operated in relation to the Father in his earthly
ministry, we see that we are called to operate in precisely the
same way. If the Father wants that mountain moved through
you or me, and we are the obedient and faithful instruments
of the Father's will, *that mountain is moving.* We don't have
to know how it would happen; all we need to do is assume
a posture of complete surrender to the will of the Father at

South Carolina. This quotation was one of her favorites. She died of can-
cer in 2005 and was a tremendous loss to her Christian community of faith.
For a white boy in the middle of a black congregation that I visited several
times, she reflected the truth and love of God as well as anyone I have ever
known. I am sure those who were fortunate enough to have known her
miss her deeply. When she would be putting strong words of admonition to
her congregation, she would often say, "Now, I'm preachin', I ain't fussin'."
Oh, she was a corker.

every moment of every day and *pay attention*. God may never ask you or me to move a mountain, walk on water, or raise the dead, but we are called to be ready, if for some reason he does. This posture is the very essence of life itself.

So the question challenges us to find the balance between the deep theological differences and the more clearly manifested sameness. It is in the differences that we find the ultimate nature of the events of the Incarnation. If we say that Jesus was the alpha and the omega, the beginning and the end, that penultimate position receives its validity from the differences. On the other hand, if we are looking for the model that is presented to us as ultimate and final, we must look at the sameness. Notice I am avoiding the word "similarities," because that gives a little too much wiggle room. He is not similar to us in his humanity, he is just exactly the same as us. To understand the role of the differences and the sameness is really to understand the power of the Incarnation to save us from a shabby excuse of a life and offer us the ultimate possibility of a life: the eternal life of God full of love, truth, integrity, peace, and joy.

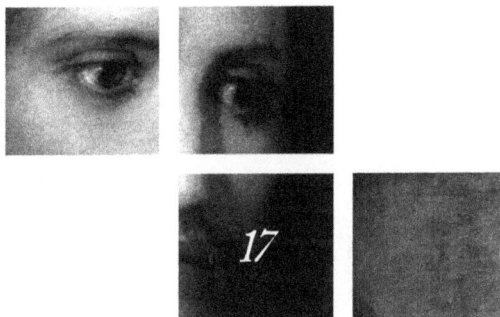

The Face of Christ

*If someone saw in you the goodness of Jesus and fell down
on their knees and said, "My Lord and my God," what would be
your response?*

The last two questions are undoubtedly the most radical
and require the most intimate and bold understanding
of the Incarnation. Interestingly enough, since we have already covered so much territory, the answers to these final
questions should really not surprise or shock us. Let us first
lay out two possible positions on this question: on the one
hand, one might understandably be put off by the comparison of one's own humanity and Jesus' divinity and respond,
"Get up, you idolatrous fool!" On the other hand, being challenged to take seriously the call to show the face of Christ
to the world, one might try to find some less reactionary response. Let's look at these two positions in some detail.

Why might one be repulsed by this scenario? Certainly
seeing the goodness of Jesus in me would not be a bad thing.
Indeed, most Christians would hope that people might see in

them at least a modicum of the goodness of Jesus. If someone else, recognizing that goodness in you, ascribed it to Jesus in some vague way, the words of Thomas, "My Lord and
my God" (John 20:28), might be going way too far. Everyone knows I am not God. It would be pure heresy for me or
someone else to say that I am God.

In fact, in Scripture we find an interesting parallel with
Peter and Cornelius.

> At Caesarea there was a man named Cornelius, a
> centurion of what was known as the Italian Co-
> hort, a devout man who feared God with all his
> household, gave alms liberally to the people, and
> prayed constantly to God. About the ninth hour
> of the day he saw clearly in a vision an angel of
> God coming in and saying to him, "Cornelius."
> And he stared at him in terror, and said, "What is
> it, Lord?" And he said to him, "Your prayers and
> your alms have ascended as a memorial before
> God. And now send men to Joppa, and bring one
> Simon who is called Peter; he is lodging with
> Simon, a tanner, whose house is by the seaside."
> When the angel who spoke to him had departed,
> he called two of his servants and a devout soldier
> from among those that waited on him, and hav-
> ing related everything to them, he sent them to
> Joppa.

> And Peter went down to the men and said, "I am
> the one you are looking for; what is the reason
> for your coming?" And they said, "Cornelius, a
> centurion, an upright and God-fearing man, who

is well spoken of by the whole Jewish nation, was
directed by a holy angel to send for you to come
to his house, and to hear what you have to say."
So he called them in to be his guests. The next
day he rose and went off with them, and some of
the brethren from Joppa accompanied him. And
on the following day they entered Caesarea. Cornelius was expecting them and had called together his kinsmen and close friends. When Peter entered, Cornelius met him and fell down at his
feet and worshiped him. But Peter lifted him up,
saying, "Stand up; I too am a man." (Acts 10: 1–8,
12–26)

While Peter is not quite as hard on Cornelius as some
might be, we still get a similar response—a clear distinction
between the humanity of Peter and the desire of one to fall
down and worship someone they believed in some profound
way showed them the face of God. Only when we go back to
what we said earlier about giving to others what Jesus Christ
has given to us do we start to feel some kind of disconnect.
What are we to do with all this? How *should* we look to others? Well, let us first look at the alternative response and see
how we might reconcile them—or at least rationally choose
between them.

The alternative is to take our radical transformation into
the likeness of Jesus Christ seriously enough to believe that
someone might just see in us the face of Christ, and if they
saw the face of Christ and recognized it as such, would have
seen the human face of God. It is like when a great friend
of mine, Jim Morris, died suddenly, and I found myself at
a gathering of the family the night before the funeral. His

sister came across the room and I stood stunned, speechless: there was Jim standing before me. She looked so much like him that I was breathless; she looked *exactly* like him, except she was a woman. I put my arms around her and, I am sure, somewhat stunned her by my response, but I felt that I was expressing love not only for her but for my friend whom I had lost. Why would we be so taken aback if someone actually saw in us the depth of Christ's love and were moved to a state of utter astonishment? This is precisely what is supposed to happen, if we are doing what Jesus calls us into.

So how do we reconcile the clear attitude of Peter in which he feels constrained to correct Cornelius and the alternative response that appears to flow directly from our radical understanding of the Incarnation and the gift of himself that Jesus offers us? Well, maybe we can't. What we can do, however, is recognize that through a process of doctrinal development over 2000 years, the Church has clarified some subtleties that even Peter might not have grasped. Remember, the Apostles were in a process of learning throughout the ministry of Jesus, only arriving at the overwhelming truth of what had happened after he had ascended. Therefore, it is possible to say, without doing any injustice to the Apostolic tradition to which we are clearly called to be faithful, that Jesus gave us a new understanding of what it means to be human. In other words, after Jesus, it is no longer appropriate to say that we are "merely" human. Our humanity has been taken up into the Godhead and has a whole new set of possibilities—a whole new stature, if we choose to avail ourselves of that stature.

Therefore, we can give with confidence a twofold response that is perfectly consistent with Church teaching about who Jesus was and who we are called to be: (a) "Praise

God," and (b) "It is not I, but Christ in me that you see." It is critical that these two parts—(a) and (b)—work together. Our first response, "Praise God," acknowledges the wondrous gift that has been given to us by Christ—that is Christ himself. As we live more and more into the life of Christ that has been offered to us, we would hope to be confronted by those who actually recognize Christ in us. If this does not take place, perhaps we should examine our lives. After the initial response, however, it is necessary to enter into some kind of dialogue that allows us to clarify what is going on, much like when Jesus said to the rich young man, "Why do you call me good? No one is good but God alone" (Mark 10:18). What he meant here can be debated, but at least it is clear he was entering into some level of dialogue to help the young man understand what he was experiencing. We certainly are called to no less.

In the end, this question pushes us to understand our lives as a bold expression of the life of Christ. If we choose to shrink from this, we abandon the very reason God became man—the way in which the life, death and resurrection of Jesus Christ saves us and returns us to a right relationship to God. This process of taking seriously our radical transformation into the likeness of Jesus Christ involves a "trying on" of Jesus, recognizing how the conditions of our lives are similar to the conditions of his life and responding similarly. Jesus once stated, "Come unto me all ye that travail and are heavy laden, and I will refresh you" (Matthew 11:28).[53] Imagine yourself saying that. If someone were to come up to you on the street and say, "I am burdened by the cares of my work and life; can you refresh me?" imagine offering to sit with them on a park bench, sharing with them the love of Christ.

---

53   This translation is from *The Book of Common Prayer*, p. 332.

This "trying on Christ" is so fundamental to the process of transformation that it should become second nature. Perhaps this is why C. S. Lewis devoted to the subject a whole chapter in *Mere Christianity* entitled "Let's Pretend."[54]

There are, however two aspects of "trying on Christ" that we need to keep in mind. The first is that it is our only alternative. Recall the passage:

> "When the Son of man comes in his glory, and all the angels with him, then he will sit on his glorious throne. Before him will be gathered all the nations, and he will separate them one from another as a shepherd separates the sheep from the goats, and he will place the sheep at his right hand, but the goats at the left. Then the King will say to those at his right hand, 'Come, O blessed of my Father, inherit the kingdom prepared for you from the foundation of the world; for I was hungry and you gave me food, I was thirsty and you gave me drink, I was a stranger and you welcomed me, I was naked and you clothed me, I was sick and you visited me, I was in prison and you came to me.' Then the righteous will answer him, 'Lord, when did we see thee hungry and feed thee, or thirsty and give thee drink? And when did we see thee a stranger and welcome thee, or naked and clothe thee? And when did we see thee sick or in prison and visit thee?' And the King will answer them, 'Truly, I say to you, as you did it to one of the least of these my brethren, you did it to me.' Then he will say to those

---

54 Barbour and Company, 1952, Westwood, NJ, p. 159.

at his left hand, 'Depart from me, you cursed, into the eternal fire prepared for the devil and his angels; for I was hungry and you gave me no food, I was thirsty and you gave me no drink, I was a stranger and you did not welcome me, naked and you did not clothe me, sick and in prison and you did not visit me.' Then they also will answer, 'Lord, when did we see thee hungry or thirsty or a stranger or naked or sick or in prison, and did not minister to thee?' Then he will answer them, 'Truly, I say to you, as you did it not to one of the least of these, you did it not to me.' And they will go away into eternal punishment, but the righteous into eternal life." (Matthew 25:32-46)

Jesus was clearly calling his followers to the same kind of ministry to others that he was about, but more than that, he was admonishing them that if they did not engage in such acts of love, they could have no part in him. In other words, "trying on Christ" is not just a suggestion but an essential directive. If we fail to do this, all the sacraments, going to church, singing, standing up and sitting down, praising the Lord, and all the church programs that minister to us—all of that has absolutely no meaning unless our lives are centered on "trying on Christ." In other words, as we have said so many times before, we are called to be transformed into the perfect likeness of Jesus Christ so that when others encounter us, they encounter the love and truth of Christ himself; and when they encounter the Christ, they encounter the human face of God.

The second point that must be made is that there are traps

associated with "trying on Christ." The profound surrender
necessary to do this without our egos getting puffed up is
quite a challenge. If our actions ever actually caused someone
to fall down in worship (unfortunately the likelihood may be
rather remote), we would be hard pressed not to bask in our
new-found status as God for someone else. Their attention
and devotion would most likely be very intoxicating and addictive. We could make a case that most cult leaders did not
start out with the express intention to have people effectively
"worship the ground they walked on," but once that starts to
happen, it is very enticing to encourage that kind of behavior.
Recall that Jesus could not send the Holy Spirit to guide his
followers until he had left them. As we have said, the inclination to attach ourselves both physically and psychologically
to a leader who seems to fill our deepest needs and yearnings
is probably universal at some level in each of us.

The second trap is that we may start to believe what others think and start to "play God." The understanding of the
delicate balance between when and how to minister to others and when to let God work is one of the great challenges
for any Christian. When we "try on Christ," we are sticking
our necks out in boldness to do something that might look
very strange to others. We must listen very carefully for the
promptings of God (that prompting probably will not manifest itself as a clear, deep voice from somewhere near the ceil-
ing) and be perfectly supple to be willing to act or not to act.

I am reminded of a situation that occurred when I was attending a closing event at the end of a weekend-long prison ministry called Kairos Prison Ministry. One of the attending prison inmates went into an epileptic seizure, and
I found myself asking God, "If you want me to jump up,
lay my hands on him and say, 'Be healed in the name of

Jesus Christ,' say the word." I didn't hear anything, so I kept my seat. We need to know that we will make mistakes. We still see through a glass darkly and hear through a brick wall. But we are called to try to keep learning, growing, listening, and trying. In the midst of this process of stepping out while "trying on Christ," we probably will find that there is nothing funnier than a bunch of folks running around thinking they are Jesus; and yet that is precisely the call to transformation—thinking we are Jesus *in the sense that* we believe we are called to show the face of Christ to those we encounter. Perfectly surrendered to the will of God as he was.

Let us not be totally surprised or put off if it actually happens. Praise God if it does and then move on to part (b). Acknowledging how Christ works in our lives is really not any different from recognizing any gift that we have as a blessing and not an entitlement. Humility in the face of our inherent capabilities is simply the recognition that we did not confer those gifts on ourselves. The ability to sing, play the guitar, fix the toilet, or design a computer is not something that we can control. We can nurture and develop the ability, but we cannot create it. The same thing is true of the "ability" to bless others by showing them the face of Christ. This is a pure gift that we call a *grace* from God. To acknowledge that grace does not mean that we deny it or misunderstand its power to bless others. The twofold response to the question is the recognition of the gift's activity in the world and then the recognition of how we came by it. The first response of someone with an exquisite and powerful soprano voice to an accolade from others should be, "Thank you." If asked how she got there, she should answer by acknowledging the precious gift that was bestowed on her and then the hard work and help of others it took to be true to that gift.

We should do no less. The appreciation of the wonder of the reality, then the acknowledgement of the gift, and finally, if anyone is interested, the process whereby we nurtured that gift are integral parts of the way in which we show the world the face of Christ. Ultimately, if we are true to this process, we will offer the same gift to others that they too might show the face of Christ to yet others:

> . . .that God may be all in all. (1 Corinthians 15:28)[55]

---

55   This is from the King James Version. The RSV translation is "that God may be everything to everyone."

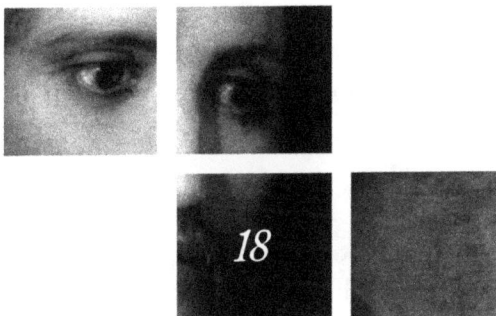

18

God

Can you be God? If you answer in the affirmative, in what sense do you mean it?

Let's be honest. Questions like this are precisely why many are put off or even horrified by *The Quiz*. If you are feeling a little uncomfortable, get used to it. Jesus did not come to make us comfortable but to move us forward into his perfect likeness. Consider the following:

> "Do not think that I have come to bring peace on earth; I have not come to bring peace, but a sword. For I have come to set a man against his father, and a daughter against her mother, and a daughter-in-law against her mother-in-law; and a man's foes will be those of his own household. He who loves father or mother more than me is not worthy of me; and he who loves son or daughter more than me is not worthy of me; and he who does not take his cross and follow me is

not worthy of me. He who finds his life will lose
it, and he who loses his life for my sake will find
it." (Matthew 10:34-39)

I have heard many say blandly, "God accepts me where I
am." My first thought is to respond, "No, honey, God *loves
you* where you are—but he expects you to *move*." In other
words, if we are not in a process of radical transformation,
we are not in the game. Maybe you have heard people say, "I
go to church to worship God." I think a better statement is
what we said earlier: "I go to church to be transformed into
the perfect likeness of Jesus Christ." Worship is an essential
part but not an end in itself. If I go to church and am not being changed, *God is not fooled.*

So, what about this "being God" business? Isn't this a bit
much? Well, let us remember the radical statements from
Chapter 15. These are all pointing us toward a radical transformation—a transformation of *being.* There is no question
we need to be very careful here, lest we fall into a huge trap;
but at the same time, we cannot substitute the radical nature
of the Incarnation with some fluffy understanding, either.

If we look at the two critical words here, they are *be* and
God. We have already articulated the two parts that we need:
a radical transformation into the eternal life of God and the
fact that this transformation is a transformation of *being.* So
when we put the two together, we get something that takes
us to the very edge—one that can only be approached spiri-
tually. We simply cannot comprehend the depth of this concept. It must be *apprehended* with the heart in prayer, medita-
tion and contemplation—the nature of which is far beyond
the scope of this little work. We can set some intellectual
boundaries for this process, but ultimately the depth of all

this will only be revealed by God.

So having placed this question in a spiritual context, we can give a concise answer. Are we called to *be* God? Here is what we have been given—access to the eternal life of God through Jesus Christ. The Church Fathers called it our *deification*, or *divinization*, or *Trinification*. This kind of transformation is not one of actions but one of *being*. As we said, this is an *ontological* transformation. Certainly we are not called to be *all of God* and operate autonomously as God does, but just as clearly we are called to *be* God in the sense that a cup of ocean *is* still ocean. It is not the entire ocean, but it is the same stuff that the ocean is made of. This is why the qualification to this question is so important. Are we called into an ontological transformation into the eternal stuff of God? *Yes*, but not into the whole infinite, wholly otherness that is the imponderable Triune God—Father, Son and Holy Spirit.

Placing those two words right next to each other—*being* and *God*—places us right smack dab in the middle of the radical transformation that has been offered to us. This is the pinnacle of the entire Gospel message. We are called by Jesus Christ to be changed down to the very core of our *being*. We are called to *be* new people. Not just to act like new people, but to actually *be* new people. If you were an amazing genius at mathematics and physics such as Isaac Newton and someone asked you to become a great ballet dancer, we would think they were crazy, because this would be contrary to who you were created to *be*. If you were a great operatic tenor like Luciano Pavarotti and someone asked you to become a great football quarterback, we would think they were crazy for the same reason. If you were a great leader like Indira Gandhi, and someone asked you to become an — well, you get the idea. This is, however, the kind of radical transformation Jesus is asking of us. Not to become something different from who we were created to be, but to be transformed so radically from the way in which we exhibit our God-given gifts that, from a spiritual point of view, it would be like Pavarotti throwing a 60-yard touchdown pass to win the Super Bowl and being mistaken for Joe Montana, or Newton doing huge *grand jetés* across the stage at Covent Garden and being mistaken for Mikhail Baryshnikov. Our transformation is not any less radical, because we are asked to be mistaken for Jesus Christ himself. This whole discussion looks remarkably like the issue addressed in the last chapter. In fact, if we are mistaken for Jesus Christ, who we believe was the Son of God, the second person of the Trinity, God in human form, then we are being mistaken for God in some profound sense. But the transformation is not just in outward appearance but deep down into our very being. There simply is no more radical transformation possible. If nothing is deeper than our own being and nothing is greater than the being of God, then Jesus was saying that we were to be transformed into God—in some sense. Granted, we need to be very careful here, and we may only start to understand this mystery at a deeply spiritual level.

Recall the following quotations by some of the Church Fathers:

> "The word became man in order to make us what he is himself." (Irenaeus)

> "He became man that we might become divine." (Athanasius)

> "A firm and trustworthy basis for hope of the

deification of human nature is God's incarnation, which makes of man a god in the same measure as God himself became man." (Maximus the Confessor)

"The only begotten Son of God, wishing to enable us to share in his divinity, assumed our nature, so that by becoming man, he might make men gods." (Thomas Aquinas)

While we must approach unpacking these quotations gingerly and understand that they are easily misinterpreted, it should at least be obvious that the authors saw the transformation offered to us as the most radical transformation possible. They were not saying that we are called to be changed into autonomous "gods" in the sense that most of us would understand the term, and their true meaning may be obscured in translation. If one sees these statements in the context of their total theological writings, they were saying precisely what we have been talking about—a radical transformation of *being* into a life that reflects and participates fully in the eternal life of *God*.

Why would we even want to tread on such dangerous ground? What good is it to understand our lives in terms of such a radical transformation? Well, there is some good news and some bad news. The Good News of the Gospel is that our lives can be filled with the love and truth that is God— just as Jesus' was. We have been offered the peace of God which passes all understanding. The living of the life of God and the sharing of it with others *is life itself.* Anything else is a shabby knock off of the real thing, which falls apart because the colors run and the stitching rots and the material disintegrates. To take this knock off for the real thing cheats us out of—well, the real thing. And to pawn off this fake to others cheats them too. Recall the words of Polonius admonishing Ophelia to be careful in her dealings with Prince Hamlet:

> *Ophelia.* He hath, my lord, of late made many tenders of his affection to me.
>
> *Polonius.* Affection? Pooh! You speak like a green girl, unsifted in such perilous circumstance. Do you believe his tenders, as you call them?
>
> *Ophelia.* I do not know, my lord, what I should think.
>
> *Polonius.* Marry, I will teach you. Think yourself a baby that you have ta'en these tenders for true pay which are not sterling.[56]

Ah, "true pay which are *not* sterling." To confuse that which is fake from that which is "true pay" is the challenge of our lives. Which aspects are sterling and which aspects are a shabby knock off? The only way we can discern the difference is to have a teacher—one who can point us in the right direction. In the case of Ophelia, it was her father Polonius, although some might question his motives. In our case, it is Jesus Christ who teaches us how to tell sterling from pot metal.

Consider the following:

---

56 Shakespeare, William, *Hamlet*, Act I, Scene iii, Line 99.

"You are the salt of the earth; but if salt has lost its taste, how shall its saltiness be restored? It is no longer good for anything except to be thrown out and trodden under foot by men." (Matthew 5:13)

Salt was the "sterling" of the old world. From it we get the word "salary," since Roman soldiers were often paid in salt or at least in money that was often used to buy salt. Salt was used to preserve food, a critical part of survival in early civilizations. To be "worth your salt" was to be a valuable contributing member of the Roman cohort. Thus, to be the salt of the earth was to be of precious value and a benchmark for assessing the value of other things. This quotation not only points to the followers of Jesus as "the salt of the earth," but also is very clear about their value if they lose their saltiness. In other words, we are not called to participate in a shabby, knock-off of life. We are not called to take this knock-off as true pay, sterling or salt. This is why we care what *true pay* looks like.

If we take seriously that we are called to show the light of Christ and be the salt of the earth, then we have life eternal—*right now*—the eternal life that *is* God. The bad news, some might think, is that it is not an easy journey. Some old things must die for other things to live and flourish—even old things we might hold as "sacred." Recall what Jesus says to the young man:

Jesus said to him, "If you would be perfect, go, sell what you possess and give to the poor, and you will have treasure in heaven; and come, follow me." (Matthew 19:21)

He is really asking the man to give up those things that get in his way—his attachments. These attachments, as we have said, can take on many forms: material things, people, lifestyles, and so forth. This process of taking on some things and giving up others is very similar to the way we grow during our lives even without any larger picture of a spiritual nature. We get toys that we cherish for a year or so, and then we outgrow them. We get clothes that we really like and wear until our parents question our sanity, and then we either outgrow them or simply lose interest and move on to something else. We have friends for a period of time and then move on because of a spat or because our interests diverge. Life in its most basic form is a process of taking on and giving up, so why would we be surprised if Jesus asks us to take on his own life and give up the life of the cheap knock-off? The trick is to see how this process of moving toward the eternal life of God and showing it to others is the very core of life itself. It is not some add on but really who we were created to be. Our faith tells us that this journey is the only one worth traveling. This life is the only one worth living.

Final Thoughts

So how do all these pieces fit together? The fundamental organizing principle of the Incarnation is the idea that Jesus Christ came to transform us into what he himself *was*. Because he takes our humanity back with him into the Trinity, we can now say that Jesus Christ came to transform us into what he himself *is*. We dwell on who he was when in his earthly mission because that is what we saw and experienced—the human face of God. His actions and his mind, the mind in which dwelled the highest form of love and truth—the love and truth of God—form not only a model for our lives but the means by which we can access that model.

Here the word "sacrament" is of great power. Some would say a sacrament is "an outward and visible sign of an inward and spiritual grace"—a sign of a gift from God. The Catholic definition takes it a step further. Here a sacrament is an *efficacious* sign. In other words, the sign not only points toward the gift, but also brings the gift about and allows us to participate in it. It is like saying that not only is the flag on the mailbox a sign to the postman of some mail inside, but *the flag put it there*. Here we have two kinds of efficacy: the efficacy of the mail itself—it brings information to those to whom it is being sent—and the efficacy of the flag—it somehow participates in the very presence of the mail. This is how the sacraments work. They not only point toward a grace that itself is deemed to be efficacious, but also are deemed to be efficacious themselves, in that they participate in effecting the grace. What is the point here? In the sense described above, Jesus himself is a sacrament.

Jesus not only points us toward the life God intends for us by being the perfect model of humanity, but is also the means for accessing that life. He is the greatest sacrament the world has ever been offered. Without a radical transformation of being that can only take place through the posture of a completely surrendered faith, we not only cannot live what we see, we cannot even see what we seek when it is right in front of us. It is like being blind toward the deepest reality of life while being able to see the trivial, meaningless aspects of human existence.

All these pieces fit together to point us toward a radical transformation *into the perfect likeness of Jesus Christ*, so that when someone sees us, they see Jesus, and when they see Jesus, they see the human face of God. In fact, what we see is not a static image but a relationship of love. We see Christ in each other as we relate to each other in love. I recently spent a weekend in Aspen, Colorado at the Aspen Music Festival. I happened to have some time from rehearsals and took the bus to the Maroon Bells, two gorgeous mountains not far from town. At Maroon Lake, near the base of the mountains, I encountered a family: mother, father and two little daughters, the youngest of whom had Down Syndrome. As I was talking with mom and dad, I felt this little hand press into mine. I was bathed in the undeserved, unrequested free gift of love—the kind God offers us, the kind we are challenged to offer to each other—from this little child. This guileless, simple child showed me the face of Christ, the unconditional love of God. This theme of God offering himself to us as love so that we may be transformed into that same love, shows up in both the Old and New Testaments. We hear the following from Paul's Letter to the Ephesians:

> For this reason I bow my knees before the Father, from whom every family in heaven and on earth is named, that according to the riches of his glory he may grant you to be strengthened with might through his Spirit in the inner man, and that Christ may dwell in your hearts through faith; that you, being rooted and grounded in love, may have power to comprehend with all the saints what is the breadth and length and height and depth, and to know the love of Christ which surpasses knowledge, that you may be filled with all the fullness of God. (Ephesians 3:14)

To be filled with the fullness of God is to access what Jesus Christ has brought us through the Incarnation, "the victory of God's love working itself out in our lives both for us and for those we are called to serve."[57] Pope Benedict asserts that we are "rescued by God's love."[58] We are rescued from a life that falls far short of what it can be by the very life of Jesus Christ, one that calls us into the life we were intended to lead. It just so happens that this life is not only the life of Christ but also, by definition, the life of God. Thus our goal is the life of God himself.

---

57 This beautiful, concise statement was offered to me by Fr. Gregory Carruthers, whose lengthy conversations with me have added so much richness to this effort.

58 *Spe Salvi*, Papal Encyclical, November 30, 2007.

This is radical stuff indeed, and yet is the point of the whole Gospel story. When we say the Good News is that "God so loved the world that he gave his only begotten Son to the end that all who believe in him should not perish but have eternal life" (John 3:16), we proclaim that eternal life is not simply heaven after we die, but the life of God here on earth, *right now*. So we can say the Good News is that the eternal life of God has been made available to us through Jesus Christ *right now*.

Let me offer a thought on ecumenism, the idea of the various Christian denominations getting back together. Many have asserted areas of commonality that could be the basis for such ecumenical movement. Some have suggested that the basis might be service to others. Others suggest that a fuzzy common belief in Jesus Christ should be sufficient. Others see tolerance of diversity as the key. I would assert unequivocally that the only legitimate basis for any valid ecumenism is a common understanding of Jesus as expressed in a common understanding of the Incarnation. When we can all answer basic questions concerning Jesus such as those on *The Quiz* similarly, we can start to see all other differences as window dressing.[59]

59　I will stick my neck out here and suggest that precisely the moment we see some answers as *correct* and some answers as *incorrect*, is precisely the point at which we start to see the validity of a Church with a capital "C." I am not suggesting that the Catholic Church, as it now exists and functions, is the answer. It may or may not be. That is not my point here. But I will assert, without limiting the possibilities, that some form of Church is essential to the protection and development of the faith as originally set down by Jesus and carried on by the Apostles. I will also say that a model of that Church will have built into it the capacity for change. It must be *alive* and willing to see and correct areas in which it has, let us say, fallen short of the glory of God, as well as see and take advantage of opportunities to learn and grow into the Body of Christ that Christ intended it to be.

If that doesn't change your perspective, nothing will. To walk around trying at every moment to show each person we encounter the face of Christ—full of love and truth—is not an easy task. All we can do—and all we are asked to do—is to keep trying, keep paying attention, keep listening, and keep availing ourselves of all the aids the Church offers us to help us on our journey.

One of the best reflections of the complete transformation that has been offered to us through Christ is the prayer, "Christ My Life," by August Berz:

> Jesus, I live—may it not be I who live, but rather you who live in me—as you lived in Mary taking on flesh and blood, so live in me, taking on flesh and blood in me.

> Think in me.
> Pray in me.
> Love in me.
> Suffer in me.

> Look with my eyes.
> Speak with my tongue.
> Touch with my hands.

> Forgive through me.
> Heal through me.
> Teach through me.
> Encourage through me.
> Help through me.
> Strengthen through me.

Walk with my feet over the earth, and in the power of the Holy Spirit lead all to the Father, so that God may be all in all.

Amen.[60]

May God's peace be with you, and may you be constantly plumbing the depths of the simple questions on *The Quiz* and many, many more as you journey into the full stature of Christ. But remember, you cannot do this alone. Find yourself a community of faith, share the stories of your journey, and learn from the stories of others. Pray together, talk together, argue with each other, love each other, laugh together, weep together, experience the wonder of God's ongoing bountiful gifts to us, and for heaven's sake—learn each other's names.

O Magnum Mysterium.[61]

60   Berz, August, *Mit Gott ins Heute* (With God Today), 1968, Benziger Verlag, Cologne, v.3, p. 249. The translation by Archbishop Adam Exner is, in his own words, "an adapted translation" with a bit of literary license.
61   O Great Mystery

Acknowledgements

If this were a scientific work, it would be easier to point out those who had a particular influence on the work being described here. In fact everyone I have ever encountered in any meaningful way has contributed for better or worse to my understanding of the things I talk about here. Having made this general acknowledgement, I should bow to a few who have had direct influence on this specific endeavor. First, as I mentioned in the Preface, I would like to thank Fletcher Montgomery for his courage to start the process. Without him the project might have died a quiet death. Blaney Pridgen's delightful and thoughtful response to the questions, his encouragement to use the quiz in a number of teaching settings, and his idea that I should write it up as a book were all crucial milestones in the long process from idea to execution. I would also like to thank Sr. Sarah Butler, whom I have not communicated with for many years, but who was the first to offer me Catholic answers to the questions. Her thoughtful and encouraging response to the ideas on the quiz has had a lasting influence. Fr. Gregory Carruthers was the second to offer Catholic answers to the questions. His insightful comments, friendship and encouragement have been nothing less than a miracle in my journey toward a fuller appreciation of the Incarnation of Jesus Christ.

I must also thank the folks at Samizdat Creative, publisher Caleb Seeling, my editor Mike DeVries, and designer Jarrod

Joplin for their sensitive and prayerful help in bringing this project from the initial rough drafts to a finished product that reflects in all its dimensions the powerful theme of the project. Finally I must shout from the rooftops my great debt to my sister, Penny, without whose love, encouragement and support this project could never have come to completion. Of course, it goes without saying any errors contained here are all of my own doing. I continue to grow in my own meager understanding of the Incarnation of Jesus Christ.

www.ingramcontent.com/pod-product-compliance
Lightning Source LLC
LaVergne TN
LVHW091216080426
835509LV00009B/1031